Monograph 6

AMERICAN ETHNOLOGICAL SOCIETY

MONOGRAPHS OF THE
AMERICAN ETHNOLOGICAL SOCIETY
Edited by A. IRVING HALLOWELL

6

OSCAR LEWIS

THE EFFECTS OF WHITE CONTACT UPON BLACKFOOT CULTURE

WITH SPECIAL REFERENCE TO THE RÔLE OF THE FUR TRADE

CENTENNIAL ANNIVERSARY PUBLICATION
THE AMERICAN ETHNOLOGICAL SOCIETY
1842–1942

UNIVERSITY OF WASHINGTON PRESS

SEATTLE AND LONDON

Table of Contents

PREFACE

This paper was submitted as a dissertation in partial fulfillment of the requirements for the degree of doctor of philosophy in the Faculty of Philosophy of Columbia University. I am grateful to the American Ethnological Society for having awarded this study publication in their Monograph Series.

I should like to express my gratitude to Professor Ruth Benedict and Professor Wm. Duncan Strong for their guidance and encouragement in writing this study. I am further indebted to Professor Benedict for obtaining financial assistance from the Buell Quain Fund to partially cover the cost of publication.

I also wish to thank Professor M. Herskovits, Professor F. Keesing, Professor R. Linton, Dr. J. H. Stewart, Dr. Clark Wissler and Dr. G. Weltfish for their kindness in reading the manuscript and for their valuable criticism and suggestions.

This statement of indebtedness would not be complete without paying tribute to the work of that great fur-trader and explorer David Thompson, whose "Narrative of His Explorations in Western America, etc." has become a classic on the early history of the Northwest. His work has been invaluable for this study because of the insight it gives into the changing character of Blackfoot institutions.

I. INTRODUCTION

Anthropology and History

For a period of over a hundred years (1730–1860) the fur trade was the sole medium of contact between western civilization and the Blackfoot, and had a profound effect upon the Blackfoot and other Plains tribes. Despite this, the role of the fur trade in the development of Plains culture has been neglected. Anthropologists interested in the historical problems of this area have centered their attention upon the effects of the horse practically to the exclusion of other factors. There has been little reliance upon documents in reconstructing the history of the Plains. In the case of the Blackfoot, had the documents been studied, the importance of the fur trade would have been inescapable, for the history of the Blackfoot is to be found largely in the records of the fur trade. To some extent the fur trade has been considered by anthropologists for the Woodland area, where the historical documents are more numerous and date back to an earlier period than for the Plains. In general, however, the neglect of available written history for its problems is a characteristic of present day anthropology.

Anthropology has been designated as an historical science for, like History, one of its fundamental objectives has been the reconstruction of the history of human society. But the conventional distinction between history and anthropology is that the historian works with written documents from which he derives objective chronological sequence, while the anthropologist works with ethnographical data from which he must infer these time relations. This difference in the evidence used has resulted in an essential difference in method.

Of the two major schools which have been concerned with historical problems in anthropology, the early evolutionists and the diffusionists, neither have used documentary evidence for their interpretations. The former used ethnographic data to formulate crude and sweeping generalizations of unilinear evolution, "built up of subjectively selective evidence torn out of their historical context." The latter, particularly the German school, set up arbitrary culture complexes or strata, essentially artificial constructs, and endeavored to trace the distribution of these complexes throughout the world. The history of anthropology thus presents the paradoxical picture of great pre-occupation with historical problems, and

1

no end of historical interpretations from ethnographic data, with only a minimum use of documented history.

The very concept of history and its function in anthropology has been so colored by these nineteenth century anthropologists that when their speculations fell into disrepute there was a reaction away from historical studies in general. Functionalism, with its emphasis upon the intensive study of cultures on one time level represented the new trend. While this interest in the integration and functioning of institutions has contributed to our understanding of individual cultures it has been unable to formulate any valid generalizations about the processes of social change, which is an ever-present problem.

It is a striking commentary on the present state of anthropology that archeology is the only branch of anthropology which is concerned about the history of culture change. Recent contributions in archeology indicate a new and creative approach, a departure from the interests of early archeologists who were pre-occupied with collection of artifacts.[1] While the ethnologists with few exceptions have practically abandoned the study of the evolution of institutions, the archeologists alone have had to cope with the problem.

The failure of anthropologists to deal successfully with these problems can be attributed in part to their systematic neglect of documentary material. Where they have been concerned with social change, the emphasis has generally been on the formulation of a number of refined techniques to infer time perspective. Sapir, for example, in a classic paper[2] devoted one page to the importance of documentary evidence, while the major portion of his paper enumerated the various methods of infering time, (seriation, association, and geographical distribution) followed in each case by examples of the weakness in method. Sapir visualized a very limited application of documented history for anthropology, that is, "to give the maximal and minimal dates to the appearance of a culture element, or to assign the time limits to a movement of population."[3] To show the more constructive and embracing use to which historical material can be put, we need merely cite Professor Keesing's study, in which he has recon-

---

[1] See for example the work of W. D. Strong, "An Introduction to Nebraska Archeology." *Smithsonian Misc. Coll.*, Vol. 93, No. 10; and Strong, "From History to Prehistory in the Northern Great Plains," in *Essays in Historical Anthropology in North America, Smithsonian Misc. Coll.*, Vol. 100; for a recent theoretical discussion see article by Julian H. Steward and Frank M. Setzler, "Function and Configuration in Archeology", *American Antiquity*, Vol. 4, pp. 4–11.

[2] Edward Sapir, *Time Perspective in Aboriginal American Culture. A Study in Method.*

[3] *Ibid.*, pp. 5–6.

structed early Menomini institutions from early seventeenth century documents.[4]

In the stimulating "exchange" between Kroeber and Boas in their articles, "History and Science in Anthropology," we find documented history relegated again to a minor position.[5] Despite the title neither deal with real history. Both have tacitly assumed that the paucity of historical material makes it negligible for the anthropologist. Nevertheless it is this material, largely taken for granted or overlooked, that can be of great value.

For almost every primitive people available for study today, there is some recorded history of contact with either western or eastern civilization. These records of contact are capable of much greater service than has been generally recognized by the anthropologist. The intensive search for such materials and their exhaustive and critical analysis can help bridge the gap between the disciplines of history and anthropology and thereby establish the latter as an historical science. This would undoubtedly benefit both disciplines. To the anthropologist primitive society with its greater homogeneity and simplicity, becomes more valuable as a testing ground for sociological and psychological theories when combined with a knowledge of written history. Conversely, the advantage to the historian is that the anthropologist's interest in process will help rescue the study of history from its pre-occupation with the recording of facts for facts' sake.

By its emphasis on the need for documentary history as one of its basic controls, the recent trend towards the study of acculturation is most encouraging. In setting up standards for acculturation studies, Herskovits writes,

"That all actual historical documents bearing on a given situation should be exhaustively analyzed goes without saying. Especially in the case of contact between European and non-European peoples will material of this sort prove important . . . . Information of this character has been neglected to a surprising degree—not only in studies of acculturation but also in studies of the ethnology of relatively undisturbed folk. Yet the light such materials shed on changing custom, the strictly ethnological data that they supply, since the early travelers were far keener observers than the ethnologists generally credit them with having been—and the sense of sureness in time depth afforded, are of the greatest value in the study of any civilization, acculturated or not."[6]

---

[4] Felix M. Keesing, "The Menomini Indians of Wisconsin," *Memoirs of the American Phil. Soc.*, Vol. 10.

[5] A. L. Kroeber, "History and Science in Anthropology," *A.A.* n.s., Vol. 37: 539–69; F. Boas, "History and Science in Anthropology: A Reply," *A.A.* n.s., Vol. 38, 137–41.

[6] Melville J. Herskovits, *Acculturtion, A Study of Culture Contact*, pp. 25–26.

However, most acculturation studies have employed history merely for background purposes.[7]

In areas where documentary material has been voluminous such as Africa, Mexico and Peru, the anthropologists have literally been forced to recognize and to use this data in their studies. In areas where there is a paucity of historical sources, such as the Plains, it has either been assumed that the material was too scant to warrant intensive study or it has been used as descriptive material for static distribution studies. This has been the procedure in a number of Plains studies. Smith, for example, has used documents covering a time span of about 150 years to construct a 'timeless' Plains war complex.[8] Actually there was rich material here to show the changing nature of Plains warfare. This use of historical documents in anthropology has inadvertently scuttled their principal asset—that is, an objective record of development.

The Plains area is particularly suited to studies of culture change because of the rich history of movements of peoples from outlying areas onto the Plains and within the Plains itself. The recency of these movements, many of which coincided with the introduction of the horse and gun, has fortunately placed them within the historic period.

A number of studies, based upon archeological and historical material, have established the value of the historicity of the Plains to our understanding of ethnological problems. Strong has demonstrated on the basis of archeology, the recency of the semi-nomadic hunting culture of the Northern and Central Plains.[9] Another type of study by Mandelbaum, presented in great detail the metamorphosis which occurred in Cree institutions when part of the Cree moved from the Woodland onto the Plains.[10] Other studies have emphasized the role of the horse as an agent of culture change on the Plains. Since Wissler's well-known essay, this point of view was developed in the works of Kroeber, Strong and Mishkin. Strong has shown that the acquisition of the horse was responsible for the transformation of the semi-sedentary agricultural Crow and Cheyenne to the nomadic hunting peoples of later years. Mishkin, in an intensive study, contended that the horse had an effect more profound and far-reaching than that attributed to it by Wissler, and concluded that it was the most important

---

[7] See Ralph Linton, *Acculturation in Seven American Indian Tribes.*

[8] Marian W. Smith, "The War Complex on the Plains," *Proc. of the Amer. Phil. Soc.*, Vol. 78, No. 3.

[9] Strong, *op. cit.*

[10] David G. Mandelbaum, *Changes in an Aboriginal Culture Following a Change in Environment as Exemplified by the Plains Cree.* (In press.)

single factor in the development of the Plains cultures of the nineteenth century.[11a]

It follows from these studies that time perspective is essential in a study of Plains institutions. Yet, with but few exceptions, the ethnography of the Plains has been written with little consideration of the history of the institutions described. As an example of what can be learned of the development of institutions from the recorded history of white contact, we have selected for our study the Blackfoot, a "typical" Plains tribe. The historical sources concerning the Blackfoot are not numerous but are, for the most part, well-known. Despite this, Blackfoot ethnography has been treated unhistorically. Here again, the documentary material has been used for descriptive purposes, or, at most, for the solution of limited problems such as the verification of the southern range of the Blackfoot.[11]

It is our purpose to present a developmental study of Blackfoot institutions and to show, to the extent the historical material permits, the changes which occurred in Blackfoot economy, social organization, marriage and warfare, following their contact with western civilization. Our method of procedure has, in a sense, paralleled that of the archeologist. It has consisted of 'digging' into historical records for information concerning culture change among the Blackfoot. For this purpose, we have examined traders' journals, travelers' reports, records of fur companies, government papers, and a host of secondary sources. The ethnography contained in these sources has been arranged in a chronological framework, thus resulting in a time schedule of the culture elements in the order in which they appear in the records of observers. It is inevitable that there should be many gaps and some of our conclusions are therefore only suggestive.

A few words concerning the organization of the material and the problems dealt with it in this study are necessary at this point. Western civilization was brought to the Blackfoot by the fur trade and for over 130 years the principal source of Blackfoot history was the written record of the fur trade in Canada and the United States. The intimate relation between the history of the Blackfoot and that of the fur trade has direct bearing upon this study and offers interesting contrasts with the southern and central Plains, where the fur trade was unimportant.

In the light of the significance of the fur trade, the role usually attributed to the horse as an agent of culture change must be re-examined.[12] Is the expansion of Blackfoot economy in the nineteenth century and the com-

---

[11a] Bernard Mishkin, *Rank and Warfare among the Plains Indians.*

[11] Clark Wissler, "Material Culture of the Blackfoot Indians." *AMNH-AP*, Vol. 5.

[12] See Mishkin, op. cit., pp. 5–24.

mercialism that became part of their values to be explained solely in terms of the horse? Is the horse alone responsible for the rapid spread and uniformity of Plains culture, or did the fur trade also play a part in this process? These and related problems will be treated in this study.

One other aspect of our work, related more directly to problems of acculturation, must be pointed out here. The unique geographical position of the Blackfoot tribes, situated as they were on both sides of the international line, subjected them to two influences, a Canadian and an American. This first presented itself in the differences in policy and character of the Canadian and American fur companies, and it continued in the differences in the pre-reserve treatment of the Indians by the Canadian and American governments. Finally, it manifested itself in the post reserve adjustments in Canada and in the United States.

While these conditions make a study of Blackfoot acculturation more complicated, they also make it more useful in that we can trace the role of the differential factors in Canada and in the United States and evaluate their effects upon the Blackfoot. In this paper, we shall study these effects up to the reserve period.

II. Origin and Early Movements*

The origin of the Blackfoot is one of the puzzling problems in the history of the northern Plains. Unlike the Plains Cree, the Cheyenne, Gros Ventre and Sarsi, who moved out into the Plains from surrounding regions in the historic period, the previous location of the Blackfoot has not been established. Wissler has dealt with this subject at various times. Writing in 1906 he stated, "The Blackfoot . . . presumably came out of the wooded lake area to the east into the open country of the west, as did their kindred the Arapaho and Cheyenne, where they gradually adopted the culture of the Sioux tribes."[13] Again, in 1908, he stated that it seemed certain that the Blackfoot migrated from the region of the Great Lakes, which he believed to be the center of dispersion of the Algonkian speaking people of the Plains.[14] In 1910, after a detailed examination of some of the available historical sources he concluded that, ". . . no satisfactory evidence has come to hand that the Blackfoot ever occupied other definite territory than their historic habitat, the western Plains."[15] Although this was written before the publication of David Thompson's *Narrative* (1916) and the *Kelsey Papers* (1929) it remains true today with but minor modifications.

Hyde, in the most recent study of the subject (1933) supports Wissler's earlier hypothesis and enlarges upon it. ". . . early in the 17th century the Red River country and the lands lying immediately west of Lake Winnipeg were held by Algonkin and Siouan tribes, most of whom were partly sedentary, dwelling in earth lodges, making pottery, planting corn and other crops. Among these people we may include the three Blackfoot tribes. . . ."[16] While we know that the Blackfoot had pottery[17] and a vague

---

* The Blackfoot, Blood and Piegan tribes are at present time located on four reserves, of which three are in Alberta, Canada, and one in Montana. In pre-reserve days they roamed the Plains near the foothills of the mountains from the northern branches of the Missouri to the North Saskatchewan. To avoid confusion we shall use the Blackfoot term "Siksika" to refer to the Northern Blackfoot, and the term Blackfoot to refer to all three tribes.

[13] Clark Wissler, "The Blackfoot Indians," *Annual Archeological Report* (Ontario Provincial Museum, 1905), p. 162.

[14] Wissler, "Ethnographic Problems of the Missouri-Saskatchewan Area," *A.A.*, Vol. 10, p. 199.

[15] Wissler, "Material Culture of the Blackfoot Indians," *AMNH-AP*, Vol. 5, p. 18.

[16] George E. Hyde, "The Early Blackfoot and Their Neighbors," p. 6.

[17] Matthew Cocking's Journal—1772–1773, *Royal Society of Canada. Proc. and Trans.*, Vol. 1, pp. 111.

tradition of agriculture,[18] there is no evidence of earth lodges and nothing that would locate them in Red River country. Hyde's reconstruction is based upon a purely speculative identification of the Blackfoot with descriptions of a people in this area given by the early Jesuit missionaries.

In the absence of archeological evidence, any reconstruction of early Blackfoot locations and movements must rely upon their linguistic and cultural affiliations, the tradition of the Blackfoot and that of surrounding tribes, and any available historical material.

Linguistic Considerations

A basic assumption in the studies of Wissler, Hyde, Donaldson, Schultz and others is that the Blackfoot were the westernmost outpost of the Algonkian speaking peoples, and it followed quite easily that they came from the east. Although this conclusion may still be true, it can no longer be based upon the above premise, for since Sapir has shown that there is practically a continuous distribution of the Algonkian language to the Pacific coast, the question of direction of movement becomes more complicated.[19] Voegelin recently expressed the opinion that there were some close affinities between the Blackfoot language and the Kutenai to the west of the mountains.[20] As early as 1885, Hale pointed to "non-Algonkian" aspects of the Blackfoot language and suggested that they might have been derived from their early contact with the Kutenai.[21] Michelson and Kroeber have also shown that the Blackfoot language is most differentiated from the typical Algonkian forms. Kroeber writes, "The methods of inflex-

---

[18] Though Wissler found no tradition of agriculture, there is a statement made and signed by important chiefs of the Piegan, Blood, and Blackfoot in 1879 to the effect that their ancestors were tillers of the soil. See, *U. S. Dep't of Interior Annual Report*, 1879, pt. 3, p. 80.

[19] Sapir, "Wiyot and Yurok, Algonkin Languages in California," *A.A.*, Vol. XV, pp. 617–646.

[20] Voegelin writes, "The linguistic evidence which distinguishes the Blackfoot from the two other divergent western Algonquians is that we know of a language, Kutenai, which shares with Blackfoot the Algonquian obviative and some other morphological features, but we know of no language to associate with Arapaho and Cheyenne in any correlative way. Are Blackfoot and Kutenai ultimately related? If so, a point of dispersion near the Rockies is called for. Are Blackfoot and Kutenai not genetically related? If not, they have had contact in proto-historic times which permitted borrowing. Either way, the Blackfoot need to be placed adjacent to the Kutenai to account for the linguistic facts." This statement was received in a personal communication. Voegelin has a paper now in press, in which he shows "the rather paradoxical closeness of Blackfoot to proto-Algonquian despite its lexical divergence."

[21] Horatio Hale, "Report on the Blackfoot Tribes," *Report of the British Association for the Advancement of Science*, Sept. 1885.

ion and the forms of pronominal affixes resemble those of the Ojibwa, Cree, and more eastern dialects; but etymologically, it seems to differ considerably more from all other Algonkian forms than these vary from each other."[22] This would in itself seem to argue for a long separation from the eastern groups, and is confirmed by historical data which shows that the Blackfoot were the earliest Algonkian people to inhabit the northern Plains in the historic period. Kroeber has used the divergence from eastern Algonkian languages to locate the Blackfoot at the foothills of the Rockies and concludes that they were "ancient occupants of the northern Plains."[23]

Cultural Affiliations

Distinctly western traits are discernable in items of Blackfoot material culture. Among these are the sinew-backed bow, quilted leather armor, horn utensils, moccasin types, and the hand game. The sinew-backed bow and quilted leather armor were first obtained from the northern Shoshone about 1730, when the latter were still east of the mountains,[24] and as late as 1810 the Blackfoot were still trading pemmican for sinew-backed bows with the tribes west of the mountains.[25]

Of the hand game, Wissler writes, "The particular form of the button used in the Blackfoot hand game seems to belong to the west of the Rocky mountains, to the coast and southward to the plateau. . . . The Blackfoot indifference to seed and button dice tends to class them with the western tribes. Neither the Blackfoot nor the Gros Ventre seem to have used the large hoop and double darts of the Dakota, Omaha, and Arapaho. Thus, in a general way, the Blackfoot fall into an ill-defined group comprising tribes on the headwaters of the Missouri and Columbia Rivers. They seem on the whole to incline more toward the Plateau and Shoshone area, than to the Siouan or Algonkian."[26]

The case of the moccasin suggests the presence of eastern as well as western elements. The structural pattern common to the Thompson, Nez Perce, Sarsi, northern Shoshone, and western Cree, was substituted for an eastern type, while the old eastern style of decoration (U pattern), was retained.[27]

While the above material indicates that the Blackfoot were influenced

---

[22] Kroeber, *The Arapaho*, p. 4.

[23] Kroeber, *Natural and Cultural Areas of North America*, p. 82.

[24] *David Thompson's Narrative of His Explorations in Western America 1784–1812*, Ed. by Joseph Burr Tyrell, pp. 330–332.

[25] Alexander Henry and David Thompson, *Manuscript Journals*, p. 713–714.

[26] Wissler, "Material Culture of the Blackfoot Indians," *op. cit.*, p. 62.

[27] Wissler, "Structural Basis to the Decoration of Costumes Among the Plains Indians," *AMNH-AP*, Vol. 17, p. 107.

from both the east and west from the earliest historic times, it tells us little of their location and movements.

Historical Evidence

The introduction of historical material allows for more definite conclusions. A survey of the source material reveals the following data. Henry Kelsey was the first white man to reach the Saskatchewan River from Hudson Bay, and to view the Canadian Plains. From his journal (1691–1692) we learn that at that time the Assiniboine and some Cree were on the Plains between the South Saskatchewan and the Carrot and Red Deer Rivers to the east. Under the date of Sept. 6, 1691, he writes of a tribe to the west of the Assiniboine who ". . . knew not ye use of Canoes and were resolved to go to wars . . . ."[28] Mandelbaum[29] and Bell[30] suggest that these were the Blackfoot, while Morton identifies them as the Gros Ventre.[31] In any case, since the traditions of the Blackfoot, Assiniboine, and Cree all agree that the Blackfoot were the most westerly group, it seems certain that the Blackfoot were on the Plains west of the South Saskatchewan by 1690 and most probably a good deal earlier.

Our next location of the Blackfoot is more definite, for according to the story of an old Piegan chief, Saukamapee, given by David Thompson in his *Narrative*, the Piegan, the frontier tribe of the Blackfoot nation, were on the plains of the Eagle Hills, near the North Saskatchewan River, in 1730, a distance of over 400 miles east of the Rockies.[32] This would place them on the fringe of a mixed prairie-woodland region, especially in the case of the Blood and Blackfoot who were probably north and east of the Piegan.

This early location of the Piegan is highly interesting in that it would indicate that they moved into their present location in the historic period, and would corroborate the views expressed by Wissler and Kroeber that the Western Plains were but little utilized in the pre-horse period. But there is the possibility that even at this time the Piegan ranged to the mountains on inter-tribal visits. Blackfoot origin traditions are singularly contradictory and are therefore of little help. Hayden, Curtis, and Wissler have recorded Piegan tradition to the effect that they originally came from the southwest, beyond the mountains, while Grinnell and others have been told just as positively that they came from the northeast. The latter version, as we shall see, is more in keeping with the picture of Blackfoot

---

[28] *Kelsey Papers*, p. 16.
[29] Mandelbaum, *op. cit.*, p. 27.
[30] Charles N. Bell, *Journal of Henry Kelsey*, p. 28.
[31] Morton, *op. cit.*, p. 16.
[32] Thompson, *op. cit.*, p. 329.

movements in the historic period as gleaned from the early literature. However, our problem is further complicated by the evidence from tribes to the west and southwest as given by Teit.[33] This indicates that the Flathead and Kutenai who lived east of the mountains, carried on trade with the Blackfoot in the pre-horse period.[34] As we have seen, early western contact of the Blackfoot has also been suggested by the linguistic similarities to the Kutenai referred to above.

Although the western limits of the Blackfoot are not clearly defined for this early period, a review of the literature enables us to reconstruct a general picture of tribal locations in this area in the pre-white period. We know that the Piegan were being hard pressed by the Shoshones who were to the South and west along the Red Deer River.[35] Further to the southwest were the Kutenai, in the valley of the Belly River, while below them were the Pend d'Oreilles and Flathead.[36] David Thompson (1787) writes, from Piegan country near the present Calgary,

All these Plains, which are now the hunting ground of the above Indians (Blackfoot), were formerly in full possession of the Kootenaes, northward; the next the Saleesh and their allies, and the most southern the Snake Indians."[37]

This agrees to a remarkable degree with Piegan tradition as recorded by Wissler over 110 years later, and also with that of Teit for the Flathead. To the east and north were the Cree and Assiniboine, while the Gros Ventre were south of the main Saskatchewan and east of the South Saskatchewan. (See Map A.)

Within the short period from 1730 to 1745 the old habitat and tribal locations in the northern Plains were changed. The Blackfoot received their first horses from the Shoshone in 1730, and at about the same time obtained firearms and iron from the Cree and Assiniboine. Thus armed with the gun and iron for their arrows, and aided by a small-pox epidemic among the Shoshone, the Blackfoot with the aid of the Assiniboine and Cree, defeated the Shoshone at about 1733, and initiated a period of great expansion to the west and southwest. Again, Thompson explains a good deal of this.

---

[33] Teit, *Salishan Tribes of the Western Plateau*, pp. 304, 358.

[34] Turney-High's material does not fit in with this picture since he contends that the Flathead crossed the mountains for their seasonal buffalo hunts only after they had acquired the horse. See the Flathead of Montana, *Memoirs of the American Anthropological Association*, No. 48.

[35] Thompson, *op. cit.*, p. 330.

[36] Teit, *op. cit.*, pp. 304, 305.

[37] Thompson, *op. cit.*, p. 328. This agrees with Wissler's information from the Piegan. See Wissler, *op. cit.*, p. 17.

"In questioning them of their origen and from whence they formerly came they appear to have no tradition beyond the time of their great grandfathers, that they can depend on, and in their idle time, sometimes this is the subject of their conversation. They have no tradition that they ever made use of canoes, yet their old men always point out the North East as the place they came from, and their progress

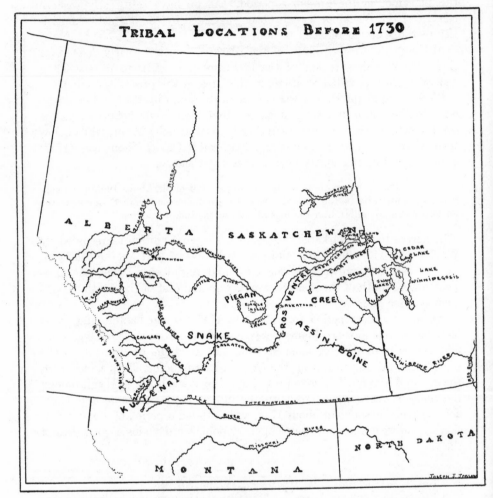

MAP A

has always been to the southwest. Since the Traders came to the Saskatchewan River, this has been their course and progress for the distance of four hundred miles from the Eagle Hills to the Mountains near the Missouri but this rapid advance may be mostly attributed to their being armed with guns and iron weapons."[38]

---

[38] *Ibid.*, p. 348.

In their push from the North Saskatchewan near the Eagle Hills, south-westward to the waters of the South Saskatchewan, they drove the Snakes and Kutenai west of the mountains. The Piegan as the frontier tribe led in this movement. They took possession of the Bow River, and south along

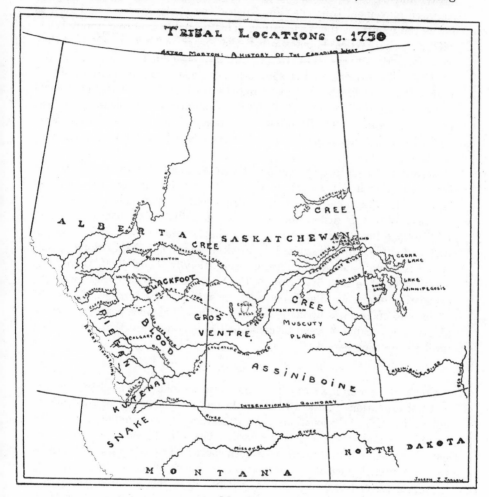

MAP B

the foothills. The Blood came to the present Red Deer River, and the Blackfoot proper to the upper waters of the Battle River, south of Ed-monton.[39] During this time the Sarsi joined the Blackfoot and were at the

---

[39] *Morton, A History of the Canadian West to 1870-71....Toronto and New·York,* n.d., p. 19.

North Saskatchewan. The Gros Ventre, driven by the Cree and Assiniboine, occupied the vacancy left by the Blackfoot.[40] The Cree pushed farther west along the wooded country of the North Saskatchewan.[41] (See Map B.)

Still another great movement of the Blackfoot took place. This was the southern movement from the Bow River down to the Missouri and even as far as the mouth of the Yellowstone. This probably occurred about 1750–1770 or earlier. When Thompson met the Piegan in 1787 he said that they were formerly on the Bow River, but now extended southward to the Missouri. The reasons for this southern movement were probably to obtain horses from the Flathead, and to find better buffalo country. The whole country along the eastern foot of the Rockies north of the Yellowstone was now in possession of the Blackfoot, who extended their war expeditions west of the Divide, penetrating far into Flathead, Nez Perce and even Kalispel country.[42]

According to Flathead tradition, it was at about this time (1750), that the Crow were first heard of on the Plains, advancing from the east and fighting the Shoshone, whom they drove out of the Yellowstone River country. With this dislocation of tribes, the tribal relationships changed. In 1730, the Blackfoot were the allies of the Assiniboine and Cree, to whom they had applied for aid against the Snakes. Again, in 1774, Cocking speaks of the Blackfoot and Assiniboine as being friendly. Until 1800, there is no evidence of Cree hostility. But as the Crees were pushed west with the exhaustion of the woodland food and fur supply, they forged out into the Plains and encroached upon Blackfoot territory. The once peaceful western plains now became a scene of continued bloody warfare that was to last until the reserve period.

Summary

Our tentative findings can be summed up as follows. The linguistic and cultural affiliations of the Blackfoot do not give us sufficient evidence to determine their early locations. The Blackfoot were in contact with tribes to the east and west for over a hundred years in the historic period, and have borrowed cultural items from both sources. The linguistic similarities to the Kutenai presents an important problem. Whether this similarity is to be explained as a result of borrowing within this hundred year period cannot be determined, and must be left to the linguists for solution. However, the historical material is clear. About 1730 the Piegan, as the frontier tribe of the Blackfoot, were on the Plains of the Eagle Hills in Saskatchewan, a distance of over 400 miles from the Rocky Mountains. Presumably,

---

[40] *Ibid.*, p. 19. Also Margry, *Decouvertes*, V1, p. 598.

[41] Morton, *op. cit.*, p. 19.

[42] Teit, *op. cit.*, p. 318.

the Siksika and Blood were to the north and east. The Blackfoot were therefore on the eastern edge of the plains near the transitional region between the forests and the plains.[43] Shortly after 1730, the Piegan, folowed by the Blood and Blackfoot, pushed west to the foot-hills of the Rockies, driving the Shoshone, Flathead, and Kutenai across the mountains. By 1754 the Piegan were on the Bow River, and by 1787 they had extended south to the upper waters of the Missouri.

---

[43] There is evidence that the Plains between the North Saskatchewan River and the Battle River was at one time a parkland region which was reduced to treeless plains by frequent fires. See A. S. Morton, *A History of Western Canada*, p. 3.

III. History of the Canadian Fur Trade with the Blackfoot

The first contacts of the Blackfoot with white culture were indirect, and came almost simultaneously from the tribes to the east and west. In about 1728 the Piegan received their first European weapons from the Crees,— several guns, a little ammunition, iron-tipped lances and arrows, some knives, and an axe. Only a few years later they acquired their first horses from the Shoshone.

Westward Expansion

Direct contact with the whites came about as a result of the expansion of the fur trade to the Canadian Northwest. Beginning with the explorations of La Verendrye in 1738, the French penetrated the hinterland to the west of Hudson Bay, and set up trading posts with the purpose of intercepting the Indian trade with the Hudson's Bay Company. The French trading posts were outside Blackfoot territory, for Fort Paskoyac, built in 1750, Fort La Jonquiere (1751) and Fort St. Louis (1753) were all east of the forks of the Saskatchewan.[44]

To counteract these French incursions which were seriously affecting their trade, the Hudson's Bay Company sent Anthony Henday inland in 1754 to induce the more remote tribes to go down to Fort York on Hudson Bay to trade. Henday was the first white man to meet the Blackfoot, (Blood Tribe).* Henday's Journal gives some account of this first meeting. After going through the ritual of smoking the peace pipe, he delivered his message, explaining that he had been sent by the great Leader to invite them to bring their beaver and wolf skins, in return for which they would get

---

[44] Blue in his "History of Alberta," p. 18, states that Ft. La Jonquiere was at either Calgary or Edmonton, in the heart of Blackfoot country. More recent authorities have shown that it was below the forks of Saskatchewan. See J. B. Tyrell, "*Journals of Samuel Hearne and Philip Turner*," Champlain Soc. Toronto, 1934, p. 23-24. Also Morton, *op. cit.*, pp. 237, 238.

* I have followed Burpee (York Factory to the Blackfoot Country, *The Journal of Anthony Hendry*, 1754-55, p. 316) and Morton (*op. cit.*, p. 19) in identifying the "Architinues" natives visited by Hendry and referred to by Cocking, as Blackfoot. However, I am indebted to Dr Clark Wissler for pointing out that there is no absolute warrant for this identification, although there is a strong probability in its favor.

powder, shot, guns, cloth and the like. A council was held on the following day and the chief gave their reply:

" . . . it was far off, and they could not live without Buffalo flesh; and that they could not leave their horses etc.: and many other obstacles, though all might be got over if they were acquainted with a canoe, and could eat fish, which they never do. The chief further said they never wanted food, as they followed the Buffalo and killed them with Bows and Arrows; and he was informed the natives that frequented the Settlements, were oftentimes starved on their journey."[45]

At this point in the journal Henday remarked: "Such remarks I thought exceedingly true."[46] The Blood evidently were aware of the trading that went on between the neighboring Indians and the Whites. Henday reported meeting a party of "Trade Indians," middle-men for the Hudson's Bay Company, in Blackfoot country, making it probable that the Blackfoot carried on trade through them.

Undeterred by Henday's failure to induce the Blackfoot to undertake the hazardous journey east, Hudson's Bay Company men made many voyages into the interior in the years following.[47] The next record of direct contact with the Blackfoot is that of Henry Pressick, 1760–61, who was sent into the country of the Blood and Blackfoot.[48] Unfortunately, we know nothing of Pressick's experiences with the Blackfoot.

Beginning with 1763, the Hudson's Bay Company was met by a new threat,—independent French and English traders from Montreal who went inland and carried their trade goods to the very doors of the Indians. They were derisively named Pedlers by the Hudson's Bay Company servants. To meet this competition, the Company sent Matthew Cocking west in 1772. He visited the Blackfoot in 1773, and again attempted to induce them to trade at Fort York on Hudson Bay but he received the same reply given to Henday twenty-one years earlier.[49]

Establishment of Trading Posts

Faced by the persistent refusal of the Blackfoot to go east and by the increasing competition of the traders from Montreal, the Hudson's Bay Company abandoned its old policy of waiting for the Indians to bring their furs to the posts on the Bay, and sent their men inland to build their own trading posts. In 1774, Cumberland House was built on the North Saskatchewan River, and two years later, Hudson's House, a little farther up the

---

[45] The Journal of Anthony Hendry, p. 338. Morton, op. cit., has shown (p. 244) that the surname appearing in the Company records is *Henday*.

[46] *Idem.*

[47] Morton, *op. cit.* p. 272.

[48] *Ibid.*, p. 252.

[49] Cocking, *op. cit.*, p. 92.

same river.[50] These posts were still outside of Blackfoot country and we have no records of trade with the Blackfoot.

With the formation of the Northwest Company in 1784, the Hudson's Bay Company renewed its efforts to establish its trade with the Blackfoot. David Thompson with a party of six was sent out for this purpose. In October 1787, Thompson set out to find the Piegan, "... to induce them to hunt for furs, and make dried provisions; to get as many as possible to come to the houses to trade, and to trade the furs of those that would not come."[51] Thompson wintered with the Piegan near the present site of Calgary, and while he gathered much valuable ethnographical data, his trading mission was not entirely successful. The trading posts were still too far outside of Blackfoot country; the nearest post at this time was South Branch House built in 1785 on the South Saskatchewan at Gardipuys Crossing on the border of the woods and Plains.

Trading posts were finally established within easy reach of the Blackfoot. In 1794, Fort Augustus was built on the South Saskatchewan with the object of drawing the Blood and Piegan southward.[52] Blackfoot country was now surrounded by a ring of posts belonging to both companies. (See Map C.)

Blackfoot Relations with Traders

Until this point the relations between the Blackfoot and whites were perfectly friendly. Henday, Pressick, Cocking, Thompson and others had wintered with the Blackfoot and had returned unharmed and undespoiled. However, beaver were becoming scarce east of the mountains and the Northwest Company once more had to expand westward. The agents of this company began to make overtures to the Kutenai, the enemies of the Blackfoot. The Piegan, who were the frontier tribe and who would bear the brunt of a strengthened Kutenai, sensed the danger at once.[53] Earlier the Kutenai had made several attempts to reach Fort George on the upper Saskatchewan but were prevented by the Piegan. M'Gillivray's journal of 1795 tells of the Kutenai trying to force their way through Blackfoot territory and attempting to bribe them with horses, but in vain.[54] The Blackfoot also succeeded in preventing the Salish and Pend d'Oreille from establishing contact with the Canadian posts until 1806, and forced the

---

[50] Thompson, op. cit., p. 318.

[51] Ibid., p. 324.

[52] Morton, op. cit., p. 511.

[53] Thompson, op. cit., p. 375.

[54] A. S. Morton, The Journal of Duncan M'Gillivray, p. 56.

western tribes to trade in a roundabout way through the Mandan and Hidatsa to the South.[55]

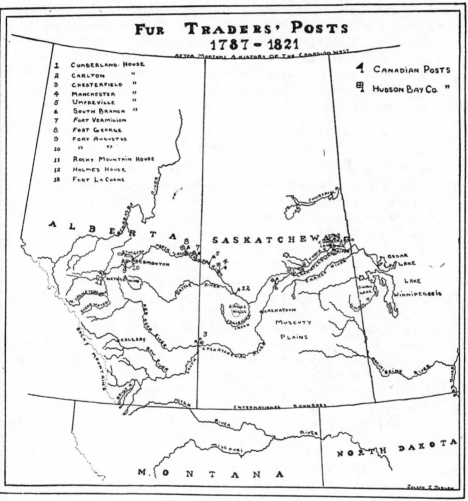

MAP C

In 1805, Thompson attempted to cross the mountains but was stopped by the Piegan, the same people who had befriended him in 1787.[56] It was

---

[55] F. Laroque, *Journal*, edited by L. P. Burpee (Canadian Archives Ottowa, 1911), p. 72.

[56] Thompson, *op. cit.*, p. 375.

not until 1807 that he managed to get across. He explains, "The murder of two Peeagan Indians by Captain Lewis of the U. S. drew the Peeagans to the Missouri to avenge their deaths; and thus gave me an opportunity to cross the mountains by the defiles of the Saskatchewan River which led to the headwaters of the Columbia River."[57] Thompson descended the Columbia and built the first Kutenai trading post. A few months later the Piegan returned from the south and learned of Kutenai House. The civil chief of the Piegan advised the formation of a strong war party to immediately crush the whites and natives to the west of the mountains before they became too well armed. Said the chief,

"They (Kutenai) have always been our slaves, and now they will pretend to equal us—we must destroy them before they become too powerful for us . . . "[58]

A war party of 300 men was formed to destroy the Kutenai post. Thompson was in serious danger but he succeeded in buying them off by sending large gifts of tobacco and pipes to the leader of the war party.[59] However, the barrier of the Piegan had important historical significance since it delayed Thompson long enough to allow the Astor party to reach Oregon first and establish a prior claim which won the Columbia valley for the Americans.[60]

Within a few years after the expansion of the fur trade across the Rockies, the balance of power among the Indian tribes had shifted. The apprehensions of the Piegan concerning the arming of the tribes to the west were indeed well founded. Formerly, the Kalispel, Spokane, Flathead and Kutenai were the easy prey of the Blackfoot. Now, supplied with firearms, they had become formidable enemies. In the summer of 1810 the Piegan suffered their first defeat at the hands of the Kutenai and Flathead, who were as well armed as they.[61] This defeat increased the hostility of the Piegan towards the whites. The Piegan would have attempted vengeance, but feared such action would deprive them of further ammunition and supplies, now doubly needed against their newly armed enemies.[62]

The relations of the Blackfoot to the tribes to the east were also affected by the Canadian fur trade. A special grievance against the traders was the belief that they were partial to the Crees, and to all appearances were more liberal in arming them.[63] To understand the seriousness of this from the

---

[57] Idem.

[58] Ibid., p. 381.

[59] Ibid., p. 383.

[60] Morton, op. cit., p. 491.

[61] Thompson, op. cit., p. 424.

[62] Alexander Henry and David Thompson, Manuscript Journals, p. 583.

[63] Journal of Duncan M'Gillivray, op. cit., p. 31.

point of view of the Blackfoot, we must remember that the differences in the rate of arming of the various tribes was crucial in determining the balance of power in this area. Here the Cree, specialists in beaver trapping, had a great advantage over the Plains Indians whose wolves and foxes were relatively worthless. This was another potent source of hostility against the whites on the part of the Blackfoot tribes, once the Cree began their incursions into Blackfoot territory. However, except for a few instances, peace was maintained at the posts.[64]

Trading at the posts continued but in an atmosphere of greater tension. The journal of Alexander Henry, the younger, under date of 1810 states, "The natives have become so troublesome that we find it is necessary to keep them at a distance while at our establishment and not allow them to come in numbers inside our principal fort."[65] The cannon in the bastion of the forts were kept ready for action, and men were stationed with loaded muskets in the sentinels gallery that surrounded the palisade when the Blackfoot came to trade. Sometimes strong arm men were on hand to administer beatings to the Indians who were suspected of making trouble.[66]

The rivalry between the Hudson's Bay Company and its competitors led the former to abandon its old policy of keeping intoxicating drink from the Indians, and by the time the posts were in Blackfoot country the Hudson's Bay Company traded liquor as freely as the others. Liquor soon supplanted other goods in desirability and became the most important single item in the trade. It provided the Blackfoot with their greatest incentive to trap. But if the liquor trade was profitable it was also dangerous. The Blackfoot were a numerous people, conscious of their power and especially violent when drunk. Consequently, the whiskey served to them was more diluted than that traded to the neighboring tribes. Whereas they would mix one part 'high wine' to three or four parts of water for the Cree and Assiniboine, they added seven or eight parts of water for the Blackfoot and it became known as 'Blackfoot rum'.[67]

In 1821 the struggle between the Hudson's Bay Company and the Northwest Company came to an end when both companies united under the name of the former. This had a very wholesome effect upon the Indians. The immediate effect was to cut down the sale of liquor to the Blackfoot to a minimum, and to stabilize the fur trade. The relations between the company and the Blackfoot Indians during this period became routine and

---

[64] In 1807 a Blood band under Old Swan pillaged and burned Ft. Augustus, and in the forties Old Fort Bow was destroyed. See Thompson, *op. cit.*, p. xc, and Katherine Hughes, *Father Lacombe*, p. 61.

[65] Henry and Thompson, *op. cit.*, p. 545.

[66] M'Gillivray, *op. cit.*, p. 46.

[67] Henry and Thompson, *op. cit.*, p. 544.

peaceful. "Inspired though they may have been by prudence and self-interest, rather than by enlightened motives of native welfare, their dealings with the Indians were marked by a sense of trusteeship and strict integrity."[68]

By 1830 the hey-day of the Canadian fur trade was over. The supply of beaver was almost exhausted east of the Rockies and the Hudson's Bay Company was forced to introduce methods of conservation in their attempts to restore the waning beaver supply. The period of expansion with its exploration and independent trappers was also over. We therefore find few journals of travelers or traders in Blackfoot country in Canada for the period from 1830–1870, the period when the Canadian fur trade was the sole monopoly of the Hudson's Bay Company. The gap in our descriptive material for this period will be filled only when the complete records of the Hudson's Bay Company which are now in the London archives, are made available to the public. However, just as our information on the Blackfoot in Canada begins to dwindle, a tremendous expansion in the American fur trade occurred, with the result that our records there are much more complete.

---

[68] George F. B. Stanley, *The Birth of Western Canada*, p. 197.

IV. History of the American Fur Trade with the Blackfoot

Hostility of Blackfoot

The first Americans to cross Blackfoot country were the members of the Lewis and Clark expedition in 1806. Through an unfortunate misunderstanding they killed two Piegan Indians. The journals of Lewis and Clark state that two Gros Ventres were killlled. However, according to David Thompson, the Piegan went south in 1807 to avenge the deaths of the Piegan killed by Lewis. This was later confirmed by Dr. Clark Wissler who unequivocally established the fact that it was two Piegan who were killed. It is certain this episode did not make for friendly feelings towards the whites.

Shortly after the return of the Lewis and Clark expedition, the American fur trade was brought to the southern limits of Blackfoot country by Manuel Lisa, who settled at the junction of the Yellowstone and Big Horn Rivers in 1807–1808.[69] He and his men were unmolested until a member of his party, Coulter, was found in a Crow camp by a Blackfoot war party. Coulter aided the Crow against the attack and killed a number of Blackfoot. The latter now considered the whites as allies of their enemies and treated them accordingly. The next time they met a party of whites the Blackfoot attacked.[70] In 1810 Lisa built a fort at the mouth of the Big Horn River. It was attacked and destroyed by the Blackfoot and thirty whites were killed.[71]

When the St. Louis-Missouri Fur Company was organized in 1808, it sent out a party of 150 trappers to the rich beaver country at the forks of the Missouri.[72] The Blackfoot considered this an encroachment of their hunting grounds and attacked them. Again in 1810–1811 trappers were attacked by the Blood and Blackfoot "who hung about constantly in the neighborhood attacking every party."[73] The trappers now armed themselves and kept up a continual warfare with the Indians. For protection

---

[69] Hiram M. Chittendon, *The American Fur Trade of the Far West*, Vol. 1, p. 137; See also *American State Papers*, Vol. 2, p. 201–202 (1834).

[70] *American State Papers, op. cit., idem.*

[71] *Idem.*

[72] Chittendon, *op. cit.*, Vol. I, p. 142.

[73] *Ibid.*, p. 330.

independent trappers traveled with the Nez Perce and Flathead, the traditional enemies of the Blackfoot, thus aggravating the situation.

The Blackfoot found a further powerful incentive to attack the trappers in the promise of rich loot in valuable beaver skins and horses which they speedily and profitably disposed of at the Canadian trading posts. An account of a raid by the Bloods in 1810 near the three forks of the Missouri tells of the variety of goods they carried off.

" . . . fine cotton shirts, beaver traps, hats, knives, handkerchiefs, Russia sheeting tents, and a number of bank notes, some signed New York and Trenton Banking Company."[74]

The journals of the Canadian traders reveal that they were aware of the manner in which the Blackfoot had acquired their beaver, for at this time, the Blackfoot still did little beaver trapping of their own. The Missouri River traders attributed much of the Indian hostility to the instigation of the Canadians. However this may be, it is certain that the Blackfoot needed little encouragement, for raiding for loot fitted in well with their own war patterns.

Up to 1831, the Blackfoot successfully prevented the establishment of trading posts in their territory in the United States, and they twice drove out agents of the Missouri Fur Company. It is not clear from the records whether or not the Piegan took part in these raids, but it is probable that they did.[75]

In 1830 Catlin observed,

"The Blackfoot are, perhaps, the most powerful tribe on the continent and being sensible of their strength have stubbornly resisted the Traders in their country who have been gradually forming an acquaintance and trying to set up a profitable system of trade. The country abounds with beaver and buffalo and others. The American Fur Co. has established itself and white trappers are rapidly destroying the beaver. The Blackfoot have repeatedly informed the traders of the company that if this persists they will kill the trappers. The company lost 15–20 men. The Blackfoot therefore have been less traded with and less seen by whites and less understood."[76]

Establishment of Trading Posts

In 1831 a group of Piegan Indians, acting as delegates of their people, signed a treaty with Mackenzie, the American trader, who promised them a

---

[74] *Ibid.*, p. 146.

[75] *Ibid.*, p. 330.

[76] George Catlin, Illustrations of the Manners, Customs and Conditions of the North American Indians, p. 52; in 1834 John Sanford, an Indian agent, reported several Blackfoot chiefs as saying, "If you will send Traders into our country we will protect them and treat them well; but for your Trappers—never." John F. A. Sanford to Gen. Wm. Clark, dated St. Louis, July 26, 1833, Files, United States Indian Office, given in *Chardons Journal at Fort Clark*, edited by A. H. Abel, p. 254.

fort of their own the following year.[77] A fort was finally established in Blackfoot country in 1833 and was called Fort Piegan, for the trade was almost exclusively with the Piegan. This fort was soon burned by a party of Bloods, "who apparently were not aware of the intentions (of the builders). ..."[78] A year later Fort Mackenzie was built and it continued to operate up to 1844, the longest-lived of the forts.[79]

The setting up of Fort Mackenzie coincided with a great change in the fur trade. Until the 1830's beaver was the most important item in the trade but after that year beaver became scarce. The American Fur Company began an extensive trade in buffalo hides, the most immediate effect of which was to improve their relations with the Blackfoot.

Much of the friendliness which followed was due also to the influence of Alexander Culbertson, agent for the American Fur Company. He had married a Blood woman and had won the complete confidence of the Indians.[80] So long as he was present, there were no hostile incidents, despite the harrowing experience of a deadly small-pox epidemic in 1837. The disease had broken out on the company's steamer when it was about to deliver a load of goods to the fort. About 500 lodges of Piegan and Blood Indians camped there, awaiting the arrival of the boat. When they were informed by Major Culbertson that the boat must be held up they were displeased and threatened to take it by force. Unable to restrain them, despite warning of the consequences, the boat was allowed to land its supply.[81] For the next two months no Indian came to trade and Culbertson went out to locate them. He met a ghastly scene of death; thousands had perished. The disease had spread to Canada and over two thirds (6000) of the Blood and Blackfoot had died.[82]

"But amid all this misery and depopulation they attached no blame to the whites. They remembered Major Culbertson's remonstrances, and felt they had brought the scourge upon themselves; differing in this respect from the lower Indians who . . . were disposed to sweep the whites out of existence as the authors of their woe."[83]

---

[77] Thwaites, *Early Western Travels Vol.* 24, p. 317.

[78] Father Points Journal (1847), Extract reprinted on p. 403 of *Chardon's Journal at Fort Clark, op. cit.*

[79] Chardon's Journal, *op. cit.*, p. 403.

[80] Lieut. James H. Bradley, "Affairs at Fort Benton 1831–1869," *Montana Historical Society, Contributions*, Vol. 3, p. 233.

[81] Chittendon gives a very different slant on this epidemic. He places the responsibility squarely upon the shoulders of the American Fur Co. officials who permitted a Blackfoot Indian to board the steamer at St. Peters at the mouth of the Little Missouri, and then go to his people without finding out whether he had the disease. In this way the disease was spread among the Blackfoot. See Chittendon, *op. cit.*, Vol. 2, p. 626.

[82] Bradley, *op. cit.*, p. 225.

[83] *Ibid.*, p. 226.

In 1842 an unfortunate change took place at the fort. Culbertson was called away and the fort was now placed in the hands of Chardon and Harvey, who promptly attacked a band of Bloods. Chardon and Harvey planned to massacre the Indians in revenge for the death of a colored servant. They invited the unsuspecting Blackfoot to trade and fired into them as they arrived, killing and later scalping thirty Indians.[84] In retaliation the fort was burned and all trading ceased until 1844, when Culbertson was sent back to patch matters up.[85] Culbertson again succeeded in pacifying the Indians and the American Fur Company continued its trade well into the 1870's with but few hostilities.

---

[84] Accounts differ as to number of Blackfoot killed. Compare Chittendon, *op. cit.*, pp. 373, 694–695, with Larpenteur, *Forty Years a Fur Trader on the Upper Missouri*, pp. 144, 216.

[85] Bradley, *op. cit.*, pp. 233–237.

V. Comparison of the Fur Trade with the Blackfoot in Canada and the United States

The Canadian fur trade with the Blackfoot had been going on for over sixty years before the first American trading post was built in Blackfoot country. The major part of this period was characterized by an absence of conflict. However, from the start, Blackfoot relations with the whites in the United States were marked by hostility and open conflict. A number of historical factors combined to bring this about.

The first American contact with the Blackfoot came at a most inopportune time. The Blackfoot had just had their first break with the Canadian fur traders in their sixty years of friendly dealings and now looked upon the whites as enemies or allies of enemies. The Piegan had warned the traders that all whites found west of the mountains would be treated as enemies in consequence of their arming the Flathead and Kutenai.[86] Undoubtedly they had also meant this to apply to their southern borders. The fact that the first Americans they met were camped with the Crow, who were their enemies, resulted in open hostilities.

More important in explaining the hostility towards the Americans was the policy of the early American fur companies of sending white trappers into Blackfoot country rather than depending upon the Indian supply. The Blackfoot resented this competition of the white trappers and attacked them as trespassers. The Canadian fur companies on the other hand, established trading posts and encouraged the Indians to trap. Furthermore a glance at the map will show that without exception the Canadian trading posts were on the outskirts of Blackfoot territory, and therefore the traders never represented a threat in the eyes of the Blackfoot.

In large measure, the greater harmony in the relations of the Blackfoot and the Canadians as compared with the Americans, was due also to the differences in organization, personnel, and administration of the respective trading companies. The American fur trade reflected the rugged individualism and lack of organization of the newly developing capitalist economy of which it was a part. In contrast, the Hudson's Bay Company with its highly centralized and efficient organization was part of the long established and smoothly functioning British Empire. The Hudson's Bay Com-

---

[86] Genevieve Murray, "Marias Pass," *Studies in Northwest History*, No. 12, p. 14 (State University of Montana).

pany had years of experience in dealing with Indians and exercised the strictest control over its employees. All Company men were subject to carefully formulated rules governing their personal conduct and their relations with the Indians. The Standing Rules of the Fur Trade summarized the policy of the Company.

"40th. That the Indians be treated with kindness and indulgence, and mild and conciliatory means resorted to in order to encourage industry, repress vice, and inculcate morality; that the use of spiritous liquors be gradually discontinued in the very few districts in which it is yet indispensible; and that the Indians be liberally supplied with requisite necessaries, particularly with articles of ammunition, whether they have the means of paying for it or not, and that no gentleman in charge of district or post be at liberty to alter or vary the standards or usual mode of trade with the Indians, except by special permission of the Council."[87]

While we can discount the tone of altruism in parts of the above, nevertheless it contrasts sharply with conditions in the American trade which had no such clearly formulated policy towards the Indians. The massacre of Blackfoot by irresponsible representatives, such as occurred on the American side under Chardon, could not have happened in Canada.

When the traders came to the Canadian northwest they attempted to deal with the Indians of the Plains in the same manner in which they had dealt with the Indians of the forest. That is, they attempted to turn the Plains Indians to large scale trapping of beaver and other small game. In this they met with little success. Among the Blackfoot tribes only a few bands of the Piegan responded to the demands of the traders. These were the bands who lived in the foot-hills of the Rockies and who had always done considerable beaver trapping. The Blood, Siksika, and remaining Piegan, refused to turn to beaver trapping. For a long time the fur trade with the Blackfoot therefore consisted only of wolf and fox skins, both of which the Blackfoot had trapped before the coming of the whites. However, with the expansion of the fur trade the Blackfoot tribes were to play an important though different role. The Plains tribes came to be the chief providers of food for the far-flung fur trade, whose numerous posts extended throughout the Woodland area, the Barren Grounds, and along the Churchill, Columbia and Frazer Rivers.[88] The Blackfoot, because of their control of the rich buffalo grounds became a major source of provisions. The fur traders of the forest regions above the North Saskatchewan depended upon those posts which were supplied with provisions by the Blackfoot, and whenever a shortage of food occurred, sent to them for assistance.

---

[87] Report from the Select Committee on Hudson's Bay Co., Appendix No. 2 (D1); *P:P: 1857 (Session 2)*, xv, 224, 260, p. 368.

[88] Harold A. Innis, *The Fur Trade in Canada*, p. 304.

The food trade consisted of large quantities of dried and pounded meat, pemmican, backfat and dried berries.

The Canadian fur trade also provided the Blackfoot with a market for horses, and horses became an important item of trade very early. The fur traders needed horses to transport supplies by land to the outlying posts. Every summer traders came up the North Saskatchewan from Fort York, their canoes loaded with supplies. They went by water as far as Edmonton and from this point the supplies were distributed and dispatched by trains of pack horses. For this purpose there were over 300 horses at Fort Edmonton alone, most of them procured in trade with the Blackfoot.[89] The American fur trade, because it was established at a later period, never provided a market for horses or so large a market for food supplies. Their main trade with the Blackfoot was in buffalo robes.

The time difference in the appearance of the Canadian and American fur trade among the Blackfoot had further significance, for the establishment of Fort Piegan in Blackfoot territory coincided roughly with a great change in the fur trade. This was the displacement of the beaver trade by that of buffalo hides, which had its greatest development in the United States. Until the 1830's, beaver was the most important item of trade. The figures for 1805, a typical year, show that the Northwest Fur Company received from all its posts the following:

> 77,500 beaver skins
> 51,250 muskrat
> 40,400 martin
> 1,135 buffalo robes[90]

The almost complete disappearance of beaver in the early thirties, together with style changes, created a demand for buffalo robes.[91] It is estimated that between the years 1833–1843 the American Fur Company traded 70,000 robes annually; the Hudson's Bay Company 10,000. In 1846, Fort Benton was established at the Marias and Missouri Rivers to accommodate the large number of buffalo robes offered by the Piegan. This site had been a rendezvous for Indians and traders since 1834, when over 2,000 robes were collected. By 1841, it had risen to 20,000 and from this date until 1870 that was the average number of robes sent annually from Fort Benton.[92] In addition, there was an extensive trade in tongues and tallow. In 1848, the number of buffalo tongues sent to St. Louis had reached 25,000.

---

[89] G. M. Grant, *Ocean to Ocean*, p. 122.
[90] Harold E. Briggs, *Frontiers of the Northwest*, p. 128.
[91] *Journal of John Work*, pp. 29–30.
[92] *Ibid.*, pp. 148–149.

The introduction of the steamboat on the Missouri in 1833 gave the American Company a great advantage over its Canadian competitors, who were still relying upon canoes and horses for transportation. Because of the difficulty and expense of transporting the bulky hides, the buffalo trade never reached the proportions in Canada that it did in the United States.

The American Fur Company, because of its advantages in transportation, were able to offer higher prices for buffalo skins. The Blackfoot planned their trading practices to fit in with their seasonal movements in such a way as to obtain the maximum prices for their furs. In the summer, they went north to the Saskatchewan, where the returns for their small peltries were highest; in winter they returned to the Marias River where they traded their buffalo robes with the Americans, who paid better prices.[93]

The differences in the values of the natives and those of the traders were a source of recurring misunderstanding both on the American and Canadian sides. The Blackfoot would not pay for drinks since they considered this "water" as due them out of ordinary hospitality. Henry wrote, "This is the cause of all our misunderstanding with them. They insist upon our treating them with their favorite liquor."[94] Again, when they gave the trader a horse as a gift they expected good payment or angrily demanded the return of the horse.[95]

Liquor was sold to the Blackfoot in both Canada and the United States, though at different periods. In Canada, the sale of liquor was greatest from about 1784 to 1821, when the competition between the Hudson's Bay Company and the Northwest Company was fierce. After the amalgamation of the two companies in 1821, liquor was almost entirely eliminated from the trade. It was at this time, however, that the American trading posts were established in Blackfoot country. With their establishment came the liquor trade on a large scale, with its usual disruptive and demoralizing influences.

To recapitulate, a comparison of the American and Canadian fur trade with the Blackfoot shows important differences in policy towards the Indians by the respective trading companies. This resulted in an initial period of hostility on the American side, in contrast to a long period of friendship with the Canadians. The American trade supplied the Blackfoot, with a market for buffalo robes; the Canadian trade with a market for provisions, horses and small pelts. The presence of competing fur companies

---

[93] *Reports of Exploration and Surveys*, U. S. Dept. of War, Vol. 1, p. 444. Report of Doty (1853).

[94] Henry and Thompson, *op. cit.*, p. 723.

[95] *Ibid.*, p. 730.

on both sides of the international line presented the Blackfoot with serious problems of adjustment.

Comparison of the Three Blackfoot Tribes

In our discussion so far we have not pointed to differences among the three Blackfoot tribes, primarily because the early material does not always mention the specific tribe under discussion. While little can be found concerning cultural distinctions, the differences in location of the three tribes and their lack of a common history have resulted in some divergences in their relations with other tribes and in their reactions to the whites.

The Blood and Siksika, the two northernmost Blackfoot tribes, were throughout their history, more closely united to each other than to the Piegan. This appears to have been true in pre-white times, for the Piegan were the frontier tribe of the westward-moving confederacy, while the Blood and Siksika brought up the rear.

The tribes were united before their common enemies, the Shoshone and the Assiniboine, but each had particular enemies against whom they concentrated their efforts. The Piegan defended the western and southern frontiers from the Kutenai, Flathead and Nez Perce; the Blood fought the Crow and, together with the Siksika, the Cree.[96] There are accounts of clashes of interest among the three tribes and of separate treaties and alliances.

Such a situation occurred in the early part of the nineteenth century after the hostile western tribes had been armed. The Piegan wished to make peace with the Kutenai, who had become a formidable enemy, but the Blood and Siksika, who were protected by the Piegan territory which was a buffer between them and the Kutenai, did not agree. The Kutenai refused an agreement with the Piegan because the latter could not speak for the entire nation and could not guarantee against transgression.[97]

Of the three tribes, the Piegan were the most powerful, warlike and numerous. They were held in awe by the others and, according to Thompson, were the leading group. He believed it would have been more appropriate to speak of the "Piegan Confederacy" than of the "Blackfoot Confederacy."[98]

According to Henry, the Piegan—

" . . . imagine themselves to be a superior race, braver and more virtuous than their own countrymen whom they always seem to despise for their vicious, treacherous conduct. They are proud and haughty and studiously avoid the company of their

---

[96] Bradley, *op. cit.*, p. 283.
[97] Thwaites, *op. cit.*, p. 87.
[98] Thompson, *op. cit.*, p. 327.

allies further than is necessary for their own safety in guarding against their common enemies."[99]

This description reflects the esteem which the traders had for the Piegan and is indicative of the manner in which the tribes reacted to the whites. It is worthy of note that the Piegan is the tribe most often mentioned in the journals, again indicating their more intimate relations with the traders. The Blood and Siksika are often described as being insolent, independent, inclined to mischief and murder and difficult to trade with.[100]

The Canadian trading companies tried to separate the Piegan from the Blood and Siksika by sending them to trade at a different post, fearing that the latter would have an adverse influence upon the Piegan. The American Fur Traders met with the same situation, suffering from the attacks and depredations of the Siksika and Blood while trading peaceably with the Piegan. The traders, therefore, treated the Piegan preferentially, thus encouraging jealousy and discord among the three tribes. This developed to the point of open hostilities on a few occasions, on both sides of the international boundary. Such an incident occurred in the United States in 1830. Mitchell, in charge of Fort McKenzie, attempted to set an example for the Blood and Siksika by presenting a new uniform and double-barreled gun to a Piegan chief, who had been faithful to the whites, that is, never traded with the Canadians. The Blood Indians present were offended and spoke loudly of their intentions of killing the Piegan. A few days later the Blood shot a relative of this Piegan chief. The Piegan chiefs immediately used this as an excuse to attack and beat the Bloods. A Piegan sought to win the support of the whites,

"Kutenapi . . . stepped forward and made a violent speech, in which he described in violent colors the offenses of the Blood Indians against the whites, and exhorted us to take vengeance for them."[101]

The greater accord of the Piegan with the traders was due to the fact that the Piegan took to large scale trapping while the other two tribes did not. This enabled the Piegan to establish themselves as an important source of beaver for the Americans. The American trader McKenzie, stated,

"The Piegan band of the Blackfoot is warmly attached to our interests. They are the beaver hunters of their nation. The other bands (tribes) traded robes and provisions principally."[102]

---

[99] Henry and Thompson, op. cit., p. 722.

[100] Henry and Thompson, op. cit., p. 530; Chittenden, op. cit., Vol. 2, p. 853.

[101] Thwaites, op. cit. In 1810, Henry reported that the Piegan frequently offered to quell the disturbances of the Blood and Siksika. See Henry and Thompson, op. cit., p. 530.

[102] Chittendon, op. cit., Vol. 2, p. 851.

Another difference among the three tribes can be traced to the fur trade. On the American side the trading posts were in the heart of Piegan country. This made for the growth of a half-breed population among the Piegan which has increased up to the present day. In Canada the posts were almost without exception north of Blackfoot country and the half-breed settlements at Edmonton for example consisted mainly of Crees. As a result the Blackfoot and Blood were less subject to the infiltration of white values and were independent right up to the last.

VI. Effects of the Fur Trade upon the Blackfoot

If we were to characterize in a word the effects of the fur trade on Blackfoot culture that word would be expansion. The key to the understanding of this expansion is the transition from an economy which produced for its own needs to one which produced for an ever-increasing market. Far from breaking down the existing Blackfoot institutions the fur trade acted as a stimulus to their development. The changes wrought in Blackfoot culture are most discernable in their material culture, social organization and warfare. Some of the more important points that will be discussed are the increase in the size of tipis, the enlargement of buffalo corrals, the higher standard of living following the introduction of elements of white material culture, the improved means of subsistence, the increase of wealth, the growth of polygyny, and the development of a commercialism which permeated Blackfoot life.

When the fur traders first came to the Blackfoot, the Blackfoot were friendly, but aloof and independent. This was due largely to their economic self-sufficiency. Unlike the Cree, and later the Flathead and Kutenai, who saw in the superior technology of the whites a guarantee against the ever present threat of starvation and became specialists in trapping, the Blackfoot scorned to turn to trapping. Blackfoot economy, in contrast to the tribes to the east and west, never became subservient to that of the whites for its subsistence needs.[103] Duncan M'Gillivray, a clerk of the Northwest Company put it very well in a passage written in 1794.

"The inhabitants of the Plains are so advantageously situated that they could live very happily independent of our assistance. They are surrounded with innumerable herds of various kinds of animals, whose flesh affords them excellent nourishment and whose skins defend them from the inclemency of the weather, and they have invented so many means for the destruction of animals that they stand in no need of ammunition to provide a sufficiency for their purposes. It is then our luxuries that attract them to the fort and make us so necessary to their happiness."[104]

With the infiltration of the labor saving devices of white material culture, and the consequent rise in the standard of living, the "luxuries" soon became necessities, and Blackfoot dependence upon the whites, though on a different level than that of the Cree, was no less real. After a time it was

---

[103] For the contrast with the Plains and Woodland Cree, see Mandelbaum, *op. cit.*, p. 38.

[104] *Op. cit.*, p. 47.

on'.y the poorest households which were without their guns, iron axes, kettles, beads, awls, blankets, etc.

Changes in Material Culture

The enlargement of the buffalo corrals and the increase in the size of tipis were a direct result of the fur trade. In order to supply the traders with more buffalo hides the Blackfoot enlarged the corrals and pounds by adding appendages in the following manner:[105]

It is possible to discern an increase in the size of tipis at two points in Blackfoot history. The first occurred a short time after the introduction of the horse. While we have no description of Blackfoot tipis in pre-horse days we can infer the limits of their size from the fact that the maximum load that could be carried by the dog travois was between 40 to 50 pounds. Since the weight of a buffalo hide was well over 50 pounds, a six to eight skin tipi would probably tax their transportation facilities to the limit. Such a tipi could accommodate between six to eight persons. However, in the earliest reference to Blackfoot tipis found in Henday (1754) or about twenty years after their acquisition of horses, Henday writes that the "leaders" tent in a camp of two hundred was "large enough to contain 50 persons."[106] From this we can infer that the size of tipis had increased to a point that would have been impossible without the improved means of transportation supplied by the horse. I think we can assume that the tipi mentioned by Henday represented the maximum size for this period and were constructed only by well-to-do chiefs.

A further increase in the size of tipis occurred in the 1830's and was related to the expansion of the fur trade and the growth of polygyny among the Blackfoot. The average tipi was made of from six to twelve skins and accommodated from six to ten people. However, in the case of wealthy

---

[105] J. Richardson, Blackfoot Field Notes, Mss.
[106] Henday, op. cit., p. 337.

individuals with large families, tipis were made of 18 to 20 skins. There were a few made of as many as forty skins which could accommodate close to a hundred persons.[107] These huge tipis contained three to four fire places. The skins were sewn together in as many as four strips and when the lodge was set up the skins were pinned together.[108] This method of construction enabled the women to set up the tipi and to load it onto pack horses.

Probably the first native item of material culture to fall into disuse following the coming of the whites was pottery. In 1774, Cocking found pottery in use among them and wrote that it was of their own manufacture.[109] It is significant that the Blackfoot were still using pottery at this time, almost fifty years after they had obtained their first horses. Soon after 1774, trading posts were established within easy reach of the Blackfoot and the latter were now supplied with kettles by the traders. When Thompson visited the Piegan in 1787 and again in 1800, he did not mention the presence of pottery, nor is it ever mentioned in the later literature. The disappearance of pottery must therefore be primarily related to the introduction of a superior substitute by the whites which could be transported without fear of breaking, and only secondarily to the greater mobility consequent to their adoption of the horse. However, for a long time the infiltration of kettles and other items was slow. In 1810 Henry wrote that "kettles are scarce", but by 1833, we learn from Culbertson's journal that there were about "one gun, an axe, a kettle, and ten knives to a lodge" and that "tobacco was extremely precious and eagerly sought for."[110]

Tobacco was another item for which the Blackfoot early became dependent upon the whites. Thompson says, "Until the year 1800 they had always raised tobacco in proportion to their own wants. When they became acquainted with the tobacco . . . brought by the traders which they found so superior to their own, they gradually left off planting it."[111] Woven rabbit skin robes and basketry are two other items that appear to have been used by the Blackfoot at one time. The reference to the former is given by Teit[112] and is based on Flathead tradition to the effect that the Flathead traded rabbit skin robes to the Blackfoot in pre-horse days. That the Blackfoot used basketry is more certain, for in 1754 Henry tells us that the Blackfoot he visited used "baskets of a species of bent" in which they served buffalo meat.[113]

---

[107] Bradly, op. cit. Culbertson saw such a tipi about 1840.
[108] G. B. Grinnell, Blackfoot Lodge Tales, p. 187.
[109] Cocking, op. cit., p. 111.
[110] Henry, op. cit., p. 724; Bradley, op. cit., p. 256.
[111] Thompson, op. cit., p. 365.
[112] Teit, op. cit., p. 318.
[113] Henday, op. cit., p. 338.

Native clothing persisted until the reserve period and later, but from the beginning the Blackfoot adopted the clothes of the whites which they regarded as superior to their own. As early as 1787, Thompson, writing of the Piegan, remarked that in wet weather leather injures the constitution and added, " . . . of this the natives appear sensible, for all those who have it in their power buy woolen clothing."[114] Culbertson, in about 1833 noted that the women were more conservative in this respect and took to cotton and woolen clothing much later than the men.[115]

Aside from guns, ammunition, powder, awls, iron, beads and the items mentioned above, the Blackfoot required little else from the traders. As late as 1855 accounts show that they were unfamiliar with white man's food and did not know how to prepare even the most common varieties. The Blackfoot had convened to make a treaty with the American government and were given gifts of foodstuffs.

" . . . they threw the flour into the air to watch it drift in slufting streams, men emptied sugar into a stream, and as it dissolved drank of the sweetened water until they could drink no more. And when they cooked the rice as they were accustomed to cook the roots, no camp had kettles enough to hold the startling quantities."[116]

In the mythology that refers to the pre-horse days the food quest looms as a serious problem. The people starve frequently and have difficulty in locating and corraling the buffalo. Yet, this probably refers only to periods of abnormal scarcity for there is reason to believe that even in pre-horse times, the efficiency of Blackfoot techniques and food preservation furnished an ample food supply for the existence of even large social groups.[117] The supply varied with the season. In the summer fresh meat was to be had in abundance and the surplus was dried and stored for the winter. The bands were almost completely immobilized in the winter by the snow and storms, and buffalo hunting was well nigh impossible. Even when snow did not cover the ground it was difficult to locate and follow the roaming herds

---

[114] Thompson, *op. cit.*, p. 353.

[115] Bradley, *op. cit.*, p. 262.

[116] Murray, *op. cit.*, p. 34.

[117] To Kroeber's recent queries (*op. cit.*, p. 77, 1940), "Could any good sized group live permanently off the bison on the open Plains while they and their dogs were dragging their dwellings, furniture, provisions, and children? . . . How could several thousand people have congregated in one spot to hold a four or eight days' Sun Dance?", the historical material gives a positive answer. An account of a pre-horse war party tells of 350 Piegan warriors fighting the Shoshone. At the conservative estimate of one warrior to every five persons we would have a group of about 1500 people gathered in one spot for a number of days. This gives a picture differing decidedly from the speculative reconstructions of pre-horse Plains conditions with its atomic social groups, "miserably poor and chronically hungry." See pp. 76–77.

of buffalo. The horse became an invaluable aid in scouting and allowed entire bands to follow the movements of the herds. In addition the horse was used as a pack animal. Formerly, when hunting parties went on foot they were limited in the amount of meat they could carry back to camp. It was the practice to take only the best cuts and leave the remaining meat to decay. The horse made it possible to transport more meat and hides back to camp. The horse therefore insured a larger and more regular food supply, lessening the contrasts between periods of plenty and periods of scarcity. However, it was the fur trade which allowed the Blackfoot to utilize the productive capacities of the horse to the full, for we have seen that the fur trade provided a market for dried provisions, buffalo hides and horses.

Marriage

It is well to recall that over 20,000 robes were annually gathered at Fort Benton. Since the Blackfoot, and especially the Piegan, were the principal traders at Fort Benton we can gauge the effects of this trade upon their lives. The increased burden of preparing provisions and tanning put new demands upon female labor and increased the economic importance of women. Polygyny grew to an extent unprecedented for the Plains.

From the journals of those who visited the Blackfoot at various intervals in the history of the fur trade we can piece together a picture of this growth of polygyny. In 1787 Thompson observed that three or four wives were not uncommon and that the greatest number any man had was six.[118] From his account we conclude that most men had only one or two wives. When Thompson returned in 1800 he reported no change. Alexander Henry, the younger, who was with the Blackfoot in 1810, reported six or seven wives as the greatest number.[119] Maximilian writing in the 1830's mentions eight wives in the case of wealthy chiefs.[120] Unfortunately, there is a great gap in the historical information on this subject until about 1870. However, tracing back to 1840 a number of genealogies gathered from informants, we have found further evidence for this steady increase of wives. Grinnell, writing of approximately the same period (1840) stated, ". . . it was a very poor man who did not have three wives. Many had six, eight, and some even more than a dozen; I have heard of one who had sixteen."[121] Denny, a captain in the first contingent of the Northwest Mounted Police in 1874, and later an Indian agent for the Blackfoot, wrote, "I have known Blackfoot with as many as twenty or even thirty women so acquired (by pur-

---

118 Thompson, *op. cit.*, p. 347.
119 Henry, *op. cit.*, p. 526.
120 Thwaites, *op. cit.*, p. 110.
121 G. B. Grinnell, *Blackfoot Lodge Tales*, p. 218.

chase)."[122] These numbers appear to be extreme but they are borne out by information recently gathered in the field by the writer. One informant told of her great-grandfather, Chief Many Horses, who had twenty wives. This was in about 1855. Our material therefore suggests that the sharpest spurt in the increase in wives occurred after 1833, a period which coincides with the increase in the buffalo hide trade both in Canada and The United States.[123]

The possession of a large number of wives was a source of wealth and was therefore cherished by the Blackfoot. The missionaries learned this when they attempted to suppress polygyny. Said a Blackfoot chief,

"Tell the priest . . . that if he wishes to do anything with my people he must no longer order them to put away their wives. I have eight all of whom I love, and all have children by me—Which am I to keep and which to put away? . . . "

The traveler, the Earl of Southesk continues,

"This chief however injured the moral force of his remarks by going on to say that his eight wives could dress a hundred and fifty skins in the year whereas a single wife could only dress ten, supposing that she was always well, and that such a loss was not to be thought of."[124]

Since wives had to be paid for in horses we must briefly consider the relation of this expansion in polygyny to the accumulation of horses and the growth of herding. We know that the Blackfoot first obtained their horses from the Shoshone in 1730. When Henday visited the Piegan in 1754 he described them as mounted but makes no mention of herds.[125] The same applies to Cocking's description of the Blackfoot in 1774.[126] In 1787 Thompson describes Blackfoot horses and though he does not specifically mention herding he states that he saw a group of thirty horses and a dozen mules at the camp at which he was staying.[127] In 1800 Thompson was again with the Blackfoot but he recorded nothing new on this matter. But in 1808 Alexander Henry, the younger, writes, " . . . some of the Blackfoot own forty to fifty horses. But the Piegan have by far the greatest numbers. I heard of one man who owns three hundred . . . . "[128] By 1833 we find that Maximilian reports as many as 4000 and 5000 horses owned by one wealthy

---

[122] Sir Cecil Denny, *The Law Marches West*, p. 51.

[123] There was a great disproportion in the sex ratio due to the increased casualties in warfare. In 1847 Father Point estimated that between two thirds and three quarters of the adult population were women. See DeSmet, *op. cit.*, Vol. 3, p. 952.

[124] Earl of Southesk, *Saskatchewan and the Rocky Mountains*, p. 155.

[125] Henday, *op. cit.*, pp. 337–338.

[126] Cocking, *op. cit.*, p. 111.

[127] Thompson, *op. cit.*, p. 371.

[128] Henry and Thompson, *op. cit.*, p. 300.

Piegan chief.[129] Although this evidence is scanty it certainly is suggestive of an increase in the size of herds. What is most significant for our purposes is that by 1833, the time when the large markets for tanned robes in the States first developed, there already existed an accumulation of horses that made possible the ensuing expansion of polygyny. This expansion in turn perpetuated and intensified the social gradations that already existed, for men with large herds were the ones who could purchase many wives, and in the exchange thereby transform idle capital (surplus horses) into productive capital (women).

Following the growth of polygyny and the increasing importance of the bride price in horses we find that the age at which marriages occurred was also altered. There was a tendency for girls to marry at a younger age and for men to marry at a later age. In 1787 Thompson reported that girls usually married between sixteen and eighteen, and men at twenty-two or somewhat later.[130] In 1885, Rev. Wilson's informants told him that girls normally married at twelve.[131] Our own informants, speaking of the period of the latter half of the nineteenth century, placed the age of marriage for girls between ten and sixteen and that of men at thirty-five, rarely at less. It is during this period that we get the first cases of child marriage. Fathers now wished to marry off their daughters as early as possible in order to realize the bride price. On the other hand, men were not chosen as sons-in-law until they had accumulated sufficient property and had acquired a good reputation as a warrior or hunter.

The increase in the number of wives brought greater friction within the household. The effect of the sororate in eliminating hostilities diminished and at the same time the contrasts between the status of upper and lower wives were intensified. The native term for a wife lower than third or fourth means slave wife, which accurately describes their status. Lower wives performed the most difficult tasks, rarely put up Sun Dances, were most often beaten and most often suspected of adultery.

Social Organization

The fur trade stimulated inter-tribal intercourse. Tribes which had little contact with each other met at trading posts with the result of much borrowing and spreading of culture elements. A case in point is the borrowing of age grade societies by the Blackfoot from some of the village tribes to the south.

The historical material offers little in the way of positive evidence for the

---

129 Thwaites, *op. cit.*, p. 121.

130 Thompson, *op. cit.*, p. 350.

131 Wilson, *Report of the Fifty-Seventh Meeting of the British Assoc. for the Adv. of Science*, Sept. 1885, p. 192.

age of these societies among the Blackfoot. If the widespread distribution of such societies in the Plains is taken as a criterion of age, then the existence of a rudimentary system of age grades is very old among the Blackfoot and probably pre-white. The fact that Blackfoot mythology refers to four basic age grades in a tale of the early days may be significant, depending upon the degree of historicity we grant to their mythology. Some Blackfoot tales are remarkable for their historical accuracy. For example, the tales which tell of their obtaining horses from the Shoshone to the west and guns from the Cree to the east are both verified by historical material.

Henday's account of 1754 suggests some policing organization, for he remarks upon the excellent discipline in a camp of 200 Piegan tipis.[132] Thompson in 1787 is the first specifically to mention a policing group. He writes of "soldiers",—young men, married or about to be married, who keep peace and order in camp and prevent gambling disputes.[133] Thompson knew the Piegan well, and that he said nothing more of societies is significant negative evidence. Our first description of Blackfoot societies as we know them was written by Maximilian in 1833. He describes a fully developed and flourishing system of age grades and their associated rituals.[134] Maximilian remarked that the Blackfoot age grades were almost identical with those of the Siouan tribes to the south.

Kroeber[135] and Lowie[136] have shown that there is a greater similarity between certain Blackfoot societies and those of the village tribes, the Mandan and Hidatsa, than between Blackfoot and Crow and Assiniboine. How are we to account for these similarities? There are at least two alternatives. Either these similarities are due to borrowing from the south through intermediary tribes, or what seems more probable, they were borrowed directly. Our knowledge of early tribal locations for our area shows that the Blackfoot had no contact at all with the village tribes. The first contacts in the historical period as shown by the literature and the tradition of the tribes themselves occurred in the eighteen twenties and thirties, when the American Fur Company established trading posts frequented by both the Mandan and Hidatsa and the Blackfoot. It is therefore suggested that the increase in the number of age societies took place at a relatively late period, probably in the eighteen thirties or late twenties. This development would therefore coincide with the period in which the expansion of polygyny and herding occurred. The borrowing of age grades

---

[132] Henday, op. cit., p. 337.

[133] Thompson, op. cit., p. 358.

[134] Thwaites, op. cit., pp. 116–117.

[135] Kroeber, "The Ceremonial Organization of the Plains Indians of North America," Congres International des Americanistes, Quebec, 1907, p. 57.

[136] Lowie, "Plains Age Societies," AMNH-AP, Vol. 11, pp. 930, 938.

at this time is intelligible in that they were an ideal mechanism for expressing and channelizing the vertical mobility which came with the increase in wealth.

Of great significance was the effect of the fur trade upon the authority of the chiefs. This varied at different periods in the history of the fur trade depending upon whether monopoly or competition prevailed. In periods of monopoly the fur trade had a positive effect, that is, it increased the prestige and authority of the chiefs. In periods of competition it had a disruptive effect, that is, it weakened the authority of the chiefs. The Hudson's Bay Company had had a well established trade with the Blackfoot. It had made it a matter of policy to deal only with the chiefs and headmen, and had conferred many honors upon them (medals, chief's coats, etc.) to enhance their authority over their followers. Since all trading with the whites had to be carried on through the chiefs and headmen it gave the latter a monopoly of white trading goods. With the increase in competition these conditions were altered. In order to gain a foot-hold the competitors of the Hudson's Bay Company brought their wares to the very tipi doors of the Indians and made their appeal to the younger men. The result of this policy is stated by Henry Jr.

"It is lamentable that the natives in general, in this country, have lost that respect they formerly had for their chiefs. The principal cause of this is the different petty co-partnerships which of late have invaded this country from Canada; the consequences are now serious to us as the natives have now been taught to despise the council of their elders . . . . "[137]

The competition between the fur companies was accompanied by sharp trading practices which the Blackfoot soon learned themselves. Franklin, writing from Fort Carlton where he met some Blackfoot in 1819, said,

"The mode of carrying on the trade (competition) is also productive of an increasing deterioration of the character of the Indians and will probably ultimately prove destructive of the fur trade itself. Indeed, the evil has already in part recoiled upon the traders, for the Indians long deceived have become deceivers in turn, and not infrequently after having incurred a heavy debt at one post, move to another, to play the same game."[138]

Another fur trader remarked that the authority of the elders had diminished to the point where fathers could no longer control the produce of their own sons.

"They are all remarkably proud of being great men but still they have little or no influence over the others . . . after making the father a chief, you are sometimes

---

[137] Henry and Thompson, *op. cit.*, Vol. 2, p. 550.
[138] John Franklin, *Narrative of A Journey to the Shores of the Polar Sea*, Vol. 1, pp. 130–131.

obliged to do the same with his son in order to secure his hunt, for the former has not the power to secure it for you."[139]

The above suggests that the instability of bands pointed out by Collier[140] for the middle of the nineteenth century may have been, at least in part, related to the competitive fur trade which undermined the chiefs' monopoly of the highly valued white trade goods. Once the young men did not have to depend upon their chiefs and elders for their liquor, for example, one of the economic bases of the chiefs authority disappeared. The prestige and authority of a chief was therefore dependent upon his generosity, and Collier considers the lack of generosity on the part of a chief as one of the most important causes for a man changing his band membership.

The Blackfoot as Traders

The Blackfoot were unusually shrewd in their trade with the whites and with other Indian tribes. They took advantage of the competition between the Hudson's Bay Company and the Pedlars, and later between the Hudson's Bay Company and the Northwest Company by demanding higher prices and better liquor. In return for horses and provisions the Blackfoot received arms, ammunition, traps, axes, kettles, awls, strouds, blankets, chiefs' coats, and liquor. The prices paid the Indians for provisions varied with the scarcity or abundance of game near the forts. " . . . generally they receive 20 balls and powder for all the flesh of a buffalo cow, or even less when the animals are numerous; but as many as 40 charges for a gun are paid them when the buffalo are at a distance."[141] The Blackfoot, with remarkable commercial perspicacity, were quick to take advantage of this and created an artificial scarcity by setting fire to the prairie in the neighborhood of the forts. Duncan M'Gillivray, writing from Fort George on the North Saskatchewan in 1794, stated, "The Plains around us are all on fire—The Indians (Blackfoot) often make use of this method to frighten away the animals in order to enhance the value of their own provisions."[142] The journals of the traders give us an interesting picture of some other aspects of the trade with the Blackfoot. Of their behavior at the forts Henry, the younger, wrote, (1810)

"They are the most arrant beggars I ever saw; refusing them an article is to no purpose; they plague me as long as they can get within hearing. Refuse them an awl, they ask for a gun . . . . "[143]

---

[139] L. R. Masson, *Les Bourgeois de la compagnie du Nord-Oest*, Vol. 2, p. 278.
[140] Collier, *Blackfoot Field Notes*, Mss.
[141] Thwaites, *op. cit.*, p. 161.
[142] Journal of Duncan M'Gillivray, *op. cit.*, p. 46.
[143] Henry and Thompson, *op. cit.*, p. 526.

"They are notorious thieves; when we hear of a band coming in every piece of iron or other European article that can be carried off must be shut up."[144]

They are also described as great bargainers.

"I have seen one of this tribe employ ½ hour in bartering a dozen wolves and twice as many Depouilles (fat on the ribs and back) and so unreasonable as to demand a Gun, Pistol, or any other article that attracted his attention for one Skin . . . "[145]

Maximilian notes this in another connection:

"The Crows in their visits and negotiations presented the Blackfoot with valuable articles, costly feather caps, shields, horses, etc. but received nothing at all when they came to the latter, by which all the Indians are incensed against the Blackfoot. In this respect the other tribes showed much more delicacy."[146]

The unusual shrewdness of the Blackfoot in their trade with the whites, their sharp bargaining, their disregard of tradition in not giving return gifts to the Crow, and the firing of the prairie to raise the price of meat were, according to the fur traders, uniquely Blackfoot, and must be attributed, at least in part, to the fact that they were subject to a competitive fur trade which made good businessmen of them.

Religion

This commercialism of the Blackfoot was not limited to their trading practices but became characteristic of many aspects of their institutions. This was especially apparent in the buying and selling of bundles. Religious bundles such as the Medicine Pipe bundle, Beaver bundle, and Sun Dance bundle were bought by an individual, usually in fulfillment of a vow made in time of misfortune. Although the bundle transfer was part of a religious ceremony, the interest of the buyer, the seller and the community was centered upon the property exchanges involved. To sell at a high price and to buy at a low price was a major objective in most bundle transfers. The buying of bundles was frequently a profitable investment, for the bundle owners received fees for the religious services they rendered to the community. Finally, some individuals bought bundles as an investment for prestige in which wealth could be displayed.

The above picture of bundle transfers applies only to the latter part of the nineteenth century. Earlier, it appears that the number of bundle transfers was less frequent and the property exchanged much smaller. In a discussion of Blackfoot medicine bundles in 1833, Culbertson says, "they might be transferred but the owners were seldom willing to surrender the

---

[144] *Ibid.*, p. 544.
[145] *Journal of Duncan M'Gillivray*, p. 46.
[146] Thwaites, *op. cit.*, p. 161.

dignity they conferred."[146a] This suggests a very different condition from the frequent buying and selling of the 1850's–1880's which is attested to by field material. Culbertson tells us that a bundle was valued at nine horses.[146b] This too, is far below the later bundle prices of thirty to sixty horses.

Judging from our more complete information of the reserve period there seems to be a direct relation between the fluidity of bundle transfers and the price of bundles on the one hand, and the number of horses. Thus, with the falling off in the number of horses on the North Piegan reserve following the depression of 1929, the bundle transfers practically came to a standstill and there was a sharp fall in the prices paid for them.

Our material therefore suggests that the greater fluidity in bundle transfers is related to the expansion in Blackfoot economy and the increase in wealth that we have already noted. We have seen that the increase in the size of herds and the growth of polygyny occurred in the eighteen thirties and thereafter. It is significant that the first mention in the literature of medicine bundles and the fact that they were sold for horses also occurs in this period (1833).[147]

This raises the question of the age of Blackfoot medicine bundles. When Thompson visited the Piegan in 1787 he made no mention of bundles and specifically observed that medicine bags were absent. It may be assumed that had bundles been present Thompson would have mentioned them because of their resemblance to medicine bags. The following passage from Thompson's journal gives an interesting account of medicine pipes, which were probably the precursors of the medicine pipe bundle.

"The natives of the forest pride themselves on their Medicine bags, which are generally well stocked with a variety of simples which they gather from the woods and banks of the Lakes and Rivers, and with the virtues of which they are somewhat acquainted. The Indians of the Plains had none of these . . . But these people must also have something to which they can attach somewhat of a supernatural character for religious purposes; and for this purpose they have adopted the Red Pipe, and Pipe Stem, which seems to have been such from old times . . . for a medicine pipe there are certain ceremonies to be gone through and a woman is not allowed to touch a medicine pipe . . . and their long pipe stems are equally sacred. These are of three to more than four feet in length, and about three to five inches in girth and well polished. Each respectable man has from three to four of these pipes which are tied together when not in use and hung on a tree; on removing from place to place the owner slings them over his back and at the encampment again hangs them up."[148]

[146a] Bradley, *op. cit.*, p. 265.
[146b] *Idem.*
[147] *Idem.*
[148] Thompson, *op. cit.*, pp. 365–366.

The statement that a woman is not allowed to touch a medicine pipe makes it quite clear that he is not referring to the medicine pipe bundle, for in the case of the latter husband and wife were the normal ritual unit. Thompson's statement about the absence of medicine bags is significant, for in 1833 Catlin gives a detailed description of Blackfoot otterskin medicine bags.[149]

While this evidence is not sufficient to determine the age of medicine bundles among the Blackfoot, it at least suggests as one possibility that the bundle complex came in between 1787 and 1833. In any case we believe that the commercialism in bundle transfers which sets the Blackfoot apart from other Plains groups developed in the period after 1830.

Changes in Warfare

Probably there have been no changes in any aspect of aboriginal culture greater than those which have occurred in warfare. These changes were brought about by the introduction of the horse, gun, and fur trade on the northern Plains.

It must be pointed out here that our conclusions for the Blackfoot are at variance with those made in Smith's intensive study of Plains warfare, and suggests that the problem of the effect of the horse and gun on the Plains may profitably be re-examined. Dr. Smith writes,

"With due consideration to their cultural importance (horse and gun) there is however, no conclusive evidence that they revolutionized war procedures. Apparently, their effect was not radically to change the existing war complexes, but to accelerate the momentum of warfare."[150]

This conclusion is based on a survey of the distribution and varieties of war honors, methods of counting coup, scalping, and motives of war on the Plains, without due regard to time perspective and diffusion. The author's "war complex" which is a static picture of nineteenth century Plains warfare, assumes a degree of stability and integration of the above elements which seems unwarranted. In view of the non-historical approach, it is not surprising that no "evidence" of vital changes was found. It is our purpose to show on the basis of the historical documents the nature of the changes in the motives, methods, and organization of Blackfoot warfare.

Early Warfare

In one of the most dramatic accounts in the literature, we are treated to a description of a pre-horse battle between the Piegan and the Shoshone given to David Thompson in 1787 by an old Piegan chief, Saukamappee.

---

149 Catlin, *op. cit.*, p. 36.
150 Smith, *op. cit.*, p. 433.

Saukamappee was a Cree by birth, and as a boy of sixteen accompanied a party of twenty men led by his father to aid the Piegan against the Shoshone.

"Our weapons was a Lance, mostly pointed with iron, some few of stone, a Bow and a quiver of Arrows; the Bows were of Larch, the length came to the chin; the quiver had about fifty arrows, of which ten had iron points, the others were headed with stone. He carried his knife on his breast and his axe in his belt. Such was my fathers' weapons, and those with him had much the same weapons. I had a Bow and Arrows and a knife, of which I was very proud. We came to the Peeagans and their allies. They were camped in the Plains on the left bank of the River (the north side) and were a great many. We were feasted, a great war tent was made, and a few days passed in speeches, feasting and dancing. A war chief was elected by the chiefs, and got ready to march. Our spies had been out and had seen a large camp of the Snake Indians on the Plains of the Eagle Hill, and we had to cross the river in canoes, and on rafts, which we carefully secured for our retreat. When we had crossed and numbered our men, we were about 350 warriors (this he showed by counting every finger to be ten, and holding up both hands three times and then one hand) they had their scouts out, and came to meet us. Both parties made a great show of their numbers, and I thought that they were more numerous than ourselves.

"After some singing and dancing, they sat down on the ground and placed their large shields before them, which covered them. We did the same but our shields were not so many, and some of our shields had to shelter two men. Theirs were all placed touching each other; their Bows were not so long as ours, but of better wood, and the back covered with the sinews of the Bisons which made them very elastic, and their arrows went a long way and whizzed about us as balls do from guns. They were all headed with a sharp smooth black stone (flint) which broke when it struck anything. Our headed arrows did not go through their shield, but stuck in them; on both sides several were wounded, but none lay on the ground; and night put an end to the battle without a scalp being taken on either side, and in those days such was the result, unless one party was more numerous than the other."[151]

We can only speculate on the degree to which this battle was typical of pre-horse warfare. The points to be noted here are: 1. The weapons consisted of the lance and bows and arrows, both iron and stone tipped; 2. The shields were effective protection against even iron tipped arrows and were used to make a temporary wall of shelter between the warriors of both sides; 3. The absence of casualties, largely due to the use of the shield.

A few years passed, when Piegan messengers again came to the Cree for aid. The account of Saukamappee continues:

"By this time the affairs of both parties had much changed; we had more guns and iron-headed arrows than before; but our enemies the Snake Indians and their allies had Misstutim (Big Dogs, that is, Horses) on which they rode, swift as the Deer, on which they dashed at the Peeagans, and with their stone Pukamoggan knocked them on the head, and they thus lost several of their best men. This news we did not well comprehend and it alarmed us, for we had no idea of horses and could not make out

[151] Thompson, *op. cit.*, pp. 328–329.

what they were. Only three of us went . . . when we came to our allies, the great War Tent (was made) with speeches, feasting and dances, as before; and when the War Chief had viewed us all it was found between us and the Stone Indians we had ten guns and each of us about thirty balls, and powder for the war, and we were considered the strength of the battle. After a few days march our scouts brought us word that the enemy was near in a large war party, but had no horses with them, for at that time they had very few of them. When we came to meet each other, as usual, each displayed their numbers, weapons, and shields, in all of which they were superior to us, except our guns which were not shown, but kept in their leathern cases, and if we had shown them, they would have taken them for long clubs. For a long time they held us in suspense; a tall chief was forming a small party to make an attack on our center, and the others to enter into combat with those opposite to them; We prepared for the battle the best we could. Those of us who had guns stood in the front line, and each of us had two balls in his mouth, and a load of powder in his left hand to reload.

"We noticed they had a great many short stone clubs for close combat, which is a dangerous weapon, and had they made a bold attack on us, we must have been defeated, as they were more numerous and better armed than we were, for we could have fired our guns no more than twice; and were at a loss what to do on the wide Plain, and each chief encouraged his men to stand firm. Our eyes were all on the tall chief and his motions, which appeared to be contrary to the advice of several old chiefs, all this time we were about the strong flight of an arrow from each other. At length the tall chief retired and they formed their long usual line by placing their shields on the ground to touch each other, the shield having a breath of full three feet or more. We sat down opposite to them and most of us waited for the night to make a hasty retreat. The War Chief was close to us anxious to see the effect of our guns. The lines were too far asunder for us to make a sure shot, and we requested him to close the lines to about sixty yards, which was gradually done, and lying flat on the ground behind the shields, we watched our opportunity when they drew their bows to shoot at us, their bodies were then exposed, and each of us, as opportunity offered, fired with deadly aim, and either killed, or severely wounded, every one we aimed at.

"The War Chief was highly pleased, and the Snake Indians finding so many killed and wounded kept themselves behind their shields; the war chief then desired we should spread ourselves by two's throughout the line, which we did, and our shots caused consternation and dismay along their whole line. The battle had begun about Noon, and the Sun was not yet half down when we perceived that some of them had crawled away from their shields, and were taking to flight. The War Chief seeing this, went along the line and spoke to every Chief, to keep his men ready for a charge of the whole line of the enemy, of which he would give the signal; this was done by himself stepping in front with a spear, and calling on them to follow him as he rushed on their line, and in an instant the whole of us followed him; the greater part of the enemy took to flight, but some fought bravely and we lost more than ten killed and many wounded; Part of us pursued and killed a few, but the chase had soon to be given over, for at the body of every Snake Indian killed, their were five to six of us trying to get his scalp, or part of his clothing, his weapons, or something as a trophy of the battle."[152]

Here we have an account of the Piegan's first view of horses which was from the unfortunate view of infantry unable to cope with the attacks of

[152] *Ibid.*, pp. 330–332.

Shoshone cavalry. The guns brought by the Cree, however, more than offset the Shoshone advantage. We are also given a more detailed picture of the organization of the war party. The large body of over 350 warriors was grouped into small units, probably the band groupings, under the direction of their respective chiefs, who in turn were led by the decisions of the war chief. The selection of a war chief by all the bands is in contrast to later procedure, as is the elaborate feasting, singing, and dancing which took place in the preliminary ceremonies and even on the field of battle. The line-up of fighters on both sides, the large size of the war party, and the bold show of numbers are also to be noted.

The great emphasis on numbers in this account brings us to one of the most important differences between aboriginal Blackfoot warfare and Blackfoot warfare of the nineteenth century. Before the gun and horse a simple difference in numbers might well decide the outcome of the battle. Large war parties were therefore essential. This necessitated band co-operation and made war a tribal affair. At the same time it called for close co-operation between individuals on the battlefield for their strength in numbers depended upon unified action. With the introduction of the horse and gun all this changed. As we have seen the few armed Cree and Assiniboine were now considered "the strength of the battle". It is this new importance of equipment as over against men (numbers) that distinguishes the 'primitive' Blackfoot warfare from that of the later period.

Motives

Economic motives were not lacking in early Blackfoot warfare but they differed from those of later years. They were principally, the defense and expansion of tribal hunting grounds, and the capture of women. Women were necessary to strengthen the tribe, both by their own numbers and as child bearers. This was a vital consideration, and had great survival value, —a point frequently appearing in the mythology. Captive women were therefore usually married and adopted into the family. The relatively few casualties in warfare must have resulted in a much more even proportion between the sexes. The almost three to one preponderance of women over men which was a "normal" condition in the nineteenth century did not exist in the days before the horse and gun.

After the coming of the whites, the capture of women received a further impetus and took on new significance, as loot, for women captives were sold to the traders. Umfreville, (1790) writes,

"In these war excursions many female slaves were taken, who are sold to the Canadian traders, and taken down to Canada."

" . . . none are spared but young girls, who are taken captive and sold to the Canadian traders . . . . "[153]

As early as 1774, Cocking mentions the exchange of two young girl captives between the Blackfoot and the trading Indians (Cree), who acted as middlemen for the Hudson's Bay Company.[154] We have not been able to determine the extent of this trade, but our material suggests that it was of some importance.

After 1830, women captives were no longer sold or traded. They were now valued by the Blackfoot as an additional labor supply to meet the new needs of tanning hides and preparing provisions for the enormous market provided by the fur trade. Here again, the old importance of women in terms of numbers was overshadowed by their new importance as aids in the acquisition of the new equipment (guns, amunition, etc.), that had become so necessary to Blackfoot life.

Loot as an objective of pre-horse war was restricted to weapons, leather armor, tools, and other small articles. These objects had usefulness but were of limited economic value, and in a sense fell into the category of war trophies.

Another motive for war was the desire for scalps and the prestige connected with scalp taking. Early in the eighteenth century an old Piegan chief tells us, " . . . we were fond of war, even our women flattered us to war, and nothing was thought of but scalps for dancing and singing."[155] Warfare had little of the commercialism of later years, but was intimately tied up with religious motives which later almost completely disappeared.

An interesting aspect of this is found in Thompson, in Saukamappee's recounting of a theological discussion concerning questions of scalping and the use of the soul of a slain enemy. A successful war party had returned with over fifty scalps. A war tent was made where all the chiefs, warriors, and mourners, assembled.

"All those whose faces were blackened for the loss of relations or friends, now came forward to claim the scalps to be held in their hands for the benefit of their departed relations and friends; this occasioned a long conversation with those who had scalps; at length they came forward to the War Chief. Those who had taken the trophy from the head of an enemy they had killed, said the Souls of the enemy that each of us has slain belongs to us and we have given them to our relations in the other world to be their slaves, and we are contented. Those who had scalps taken from the enemy that were found dead under the shields were at a loss what to say, as not one could say he had actually slain the enemy whose scalp he held, and yet wanted to send their souls to be the slaves of their departed relations. This caused much discussion, and the old chiefs decided it could not be done; and that no one could send the soul of an

---

[153] Edward Umfreville, *The Present State of Hudson Bay*, pp. 177, 188.

[154] Cocking, *op. cit.*, p. 110.

[155] Thompson, *op. cit.*, p. 339.

enemy to be a slave in the other world except the warrior who had actually killed him; the scalps you hold are trophies of the Battle but they give you no right to the soul of the enemy from whom it was taken; he alone who kills an enemy has a right to the soul, and to give it to be a slave to whom he pleases. This decision did not please them, but they were obliged to abide by it."[156]

While this concept is to be found in almost identical form among the Winnebago,[157] the writer knows of no other Plains tribe for whom it was reported. From this it would appear that Blackfoot warfare contained some elements of Woodland ideology in the 1730's,[158] but the methods of fighting differed from the Woodland man to man style, and had become well adapted to the conditions of the Plains.[158a]

The large scale warfare that was described above demanded a good degree of centralized leadership and Thompson's account of Piegan chieftainship (1787) suggests that there was a clearly differentiated tribal war chief of more or less permanence, with authority limited to war matters and war periods.

"They (Piegan) have a civil and military Chief. The first was called Sakatow, or orator, and the office appeared hereditary in his family as his father had been the civil Chief, and his eldest son was to take his place at his death, and occasionally acted for him . . . , his insignia of office was the backs of two fine otterskins covered with mother of pearl, which from behind his neck hung down his breast to below the belt; When his son acted for him he always had this ornament on him. In every council he presided except one of war. He had couriers which went from camp to camp and brought news . . . of where the great bison herds were feeding, and of the direction they were taking."

"The War Chief confined himself to war matters and the care of the camp of which he was, which was generally of fifty to one hundred tents, generally a full day's march nearer to the Snake Indians than any other camp. It was supposed he looked on the Civil chief with indifference as a garrulous old man more fit for talking than for anything else, and they rarely camped together."[159]

This comparison of the peace chief and war chief seems to attribute an equal degree of permanence to both offices. But the existence of a war chief as over against the temporary leader of small parties is suggested even more

[156] Thompson, *op. cit.*, pp. 332–333.

[157] Paul Radin, *The Winnebago*, p. 144. See his description of the four nights wake.

[158] Our only later reference to this concept among the Blackfoot is found in Maximilian. A Piegan had been killed by some Bloods and the dead man's brother made this speech to the weeping relatives. "Why do you lament and cry?—see, I do not cry! he is gone into the other country and we cannot awaken him; but at least two Blood Indians must accompany him and wait upon him there." Thwaites, *op. cit.*, Vol. 23, p. 14.

[158a] "War in the open Plains between the natives is very different from war in the woods; in the former they act as a body in concert in all their movements, in the woods it is almost Man to Man." See Thompson, *op. cit.*, p. 552.

[159] Thompson, *op. cit.*, pp. 346, 347.

strongly from the following description referring to an event in about 1750. The Piegan were eighty miles below the Bow River and were undecided whether to go further south because of their fear of the Shoshone.

"After consultation it was agreed to send out a war chief with about fifty warriors to examine the country a few days journey. The chief soon collected his warriors and having examined their arms, and having seen that every one had two pairs of shoes, some dried provisions and other necessaries, in the evening *the principal war chief* (my emphasis) addressed the chief at the head of the party; reminding him that the warriors now accompanying him would steadily follow him, that they were sent to destroy their enemies, that he must be wise and cautious and bring back the warriors entrusted to his care."[160]

So long as fighting was regularly carried on by large massed forces the war chief had a definite function. However, subsequent changes in methods of warfare affected his role. The battle described earlier in this paper which took place in the 1730's marked the beginning of a transition period which was explained by Thompson's informant. (1787)

"The terror of that battle and our guns has prevented more general battles, and our wars have since been carried on by ambuscade and surprise of small camps in which we have greatly the advantage, from our Guns, arrow shods of iron, long knives, flat bayonets and axes from the Traders."[161]

With the increase in smaller war parties so characteristic of the later period, there was a corresponding decline in the position of the war chief, who disappeared entirely by the middle of the nineteenth century when the temporary leader of small war parties became the rule. This explains a discrepancy in the literature whereby some have reported the office of a tribal war chief and others have claimed no knowledge of it. Our last reference to the war chief as described above is found in MacLeans report of 1885.[162] In all later accounts the emphasis is upon the leader of small parties.

It is tempting to draw a further inference from our last quotation, namely, that the small raiding party did not exist in pre-horse Blackfoot culture. However, in the face of the widespread distribution of the small war party in North America more evidence would be necessary for such a conclusion. It is more probable that both the pattern of the large scale warfare and the small war party existed side by side earlier, as they did in the nineteenth century. The question is really one of their relative importance. We intend to show that the horse and gun increased the use of

---

[160] *Ibid.*, p. 342.

[161] *Ibid.*, p. 336.

[162] Rev. John MacLean, "Social Organization of the Blackfoot Indians," *Transactions of the Canadian Institute*, p. 252 (1892).

the small raiding party to the point where it became the most characteristic type of Blackfoot warfare.

This change in emphasis occurred gradually. The Blackfoot utilized the large scale pattern of tribal warfare during the fifty year period of territorial expansion, beginning in the 1730's, whereby they moved across the western Plains driving the Shoshone, Kutenai, and Flathead before them. In addition to the horse and gun, we must now attribute a good part of this successful conquest to the military strength made possible by their well developed political system. The systematic sending out of the small raiding party became important only after they had established their domination of the western Plains, when continued raids for horses superseded disputes over territory.

Large war parties persisted even after the pattern of the raiding party was well established. This occurred mainly when the tribal interests were threatened, such as the attempts of the allied Plateau groups to hunt buffalo on the Plains. In 1787 Thompson wrote, "a party of about 250 warriors under the command of Kutenai Appe went off to war against the Snake Indians".[163] In 1800 the same chief, "was utterly adverse to small parties, except for horse stealing.... He seldom took the field with less than 200 warriors, but frequently with many more."[164]

In these accounts we find elements similar to those described in Saukamappee's account. In a battle between the Piegan and Kutenai in 1810, in which both sides were armed with the gun, the Kutenai formed a rude rampart with their tents, tent poles, and baggage. The Piegan attacked with their cavalry but were three times repulsed. They then resorted to their older practice of infantry fighting. About 170 men drew up a rude line about 400 yards from the enemy, and at intervals sent forty men forward to dare them to battle. They would approach to about 60–80 yards, shouting insults, calling them old women, and dancing and springing in a frantic manner so as to make more difficult targets.[165] These elements are clearly a survival of an old pattern.

Later Warfare

Changes occurred in the use of weapons following the introduction of the gun. The lance, once so important, was discarded as a useful weapon and became a ceremonial object. The quilted leather shirts that were worn for protection against arrows were of little use against bullets and gradually disappeared. The shield, while losing most of its utilitarian value became

---

[163] *Op. cit.*, p. 347.
[164] *Ibid.*, p. 370.
[165] *Ibid.*, pp. 424–425.

very important as a medicine object, deriving its power from the symbols painted upon it.[166]

The camp circle is recent among the Blackfoot. When Henday visited the Blackfoot in 1754 he came upon 200 tents camped in two parallel lines with an open avenue between them.[167] Jenness suggests that this arrangement was "very satisfactory for repelling slow infantry attacks, but not the sudden raids of mobile horsemen."[168] Undoubtedly the adoption of the camp circle was also related to their attempts to protect their newly acquired horses from raiding parties, for Maximilian tells us that horses were kept in corrals within the camp circle.[169] The origin of the camp circle among the Blackfoot may therefore tentatively be attributed to the changes in warfare consequent to the introduction of the horse on the Plains.[170]

More important, warfare had become an integral part of the new Blackfoot economy. To better understand this relationship we must consider briefly the role of the horse in Blackfoot economy.

The importance of horses can be gauged by the extensive native terminology used to describe them. The writer has gathered more than twenty terms describing the types and qualities of horses. Horses were classified according to their functions, as race horses, war horses, travois horses and pack horses; and by their special abilities, as "horses that can go long distances", "horses that can run in deep snow", etc. It is clear that horses were valued for their aid in hunting, in war and in transportation. But, in addition to their utilitarian and productive values, horses became a medium of exchange and the main form of wealth.

The accumulation of wealth, the manipulation of property, spending, buying, and selling, dominated Blackfoot life. Social position depended upon the liberal use of wealth, ostentatious display, and other forms of social investment. Every step in religious and secular ritual involved property payments, and the number of horses that changed hands in the bundle transfers, and the buying into societies was truly remarkable. The ownership of horses therefore became a major index of social status.

The ownership of horses had still further importance, for horses were

---

[166] An attempt on the part of the American Fur Co. to introduce polished metal shields was effectively blocked by the medicine men who as Bradley tells us, "would have thus been deprived of an important source of revenue." Bradley, *op. cit.*, Vol. 9, p. 282.

[167] Henday, *op. cit.*, p. 355.

[168] Diamond Jenness, *The Sarsi*, p. 13.

[169] The arrangement of two parallel lines was used in marching, as is described in Stanley's account of 1854. ". . . in less than one hour the whole encampment was drawn out in two parallel lines on the Plains, forming one of the most picturesque scenes I have ever witnessed." *Report of the Commissioner of Indian Affairs* (1854), p. 200.

[170] Idem.

used as capital, earning interest for the owner in the form of a "gift" of additional horses or equivalent property from the borrower. When a man had a number of horses over and above the domestic needs of his family, the surplus could be loaned out. With the accumulation of large herds this lending of horses became general. Horses were borrowed for use in hunting and war parties. The borrower had to give in return one half of the game killed, and one half of the loot captured.[171] In this way, owners of huge herds, who had long given up the war path, could replenish their supply of horses by frequently lending them to poor young men.

A large surplus of horses was not necessary for lending. Men who were too old to hunt and old women who had no relatives upon whom to rely, could secure food and clothing for themselves if they owned but two horses. Horses were looked upon as a source of security in one's old age, a point oft repeated to young men.

Horses were also in demand at the trading posts and were used by the Blackfoot to pay for goods, ammunition, liquor, tobacco, and other supplies. As we have seen, the Blackfoot never took to the trapping of small game on a large scale. They had few furs for exchange before the 1830's and relied upon horses almost from the start. Blackfoot horse trading was carried on as early as 1774, as shown by Cocking.[172] This need for horses, both for the tribal economy and for trading purposes, gave continual impetus to horse-stealing parties.

The organization of a raiding party was a purely individual affair. A party was organized by the man who wished to be the leader. He notified a number of carefully selected men of his intentions and arranged for a meeting at which the plans would be discussed. Participation in a raiding party was determined by rank, equipment, and the relationship to the leader. The party normally was composed of members of one band; brothers and brothers-in-law were a favorite raiding unit for they could thereby keep the horses in the family. The leader never invited a man superior to him in war record nor would such a man raid under him. Similarly, a poor man would not attempt to lead a group of wealthier men, even though they were younger.[173] A man of high status, whether it be in terms of war record,

---

[171] The rigidity of the interest concept could not be ascertained, though all informants insisted upon the fifty percent principle. Probably much depended upon the relationship of the "contracting" parties. A somewhat different arrangement is reported by Jane Richardson for the Northern Blackfoot. Here the hired men under the famous chief, Crowfoot, gave him the entire loot and catch in return for which they were fed and clothed by the chief and received some horses upon their marriage. See J. Richardson, *Northern Blackfoot*, Mss.

[172] Cocking, *op. cit.*, p. 110.

[173] A poor man, "kimataps" is one who has not or never had any valuable property or religious articles. A man with a good war record would not be called "kimataps" though he may have little or no property.

wealth in horses or the ownership of medicine bundles, would refuse to be led by one of lower standing. Not only were the poor rarely leaders, but they often had difficulty in joining a raiding party, for participation was limited to those who had the necessary equipment—a gun, powder and ammunition, a good supply of moccasins, dried provisions, protective war charms, and, when the party went on horse, a good horse.

With adequate skill, any member of the tribe could produce the equipment necessary for the early type of warfare, but the new equipment, guns and ammunition, could be purchased from the trading posts only by those who had a surplus of horses, dried provisions or hides. This put the poor at a distinct disadvantage, and was a check upon vertical mobility. This also gave a new paternalistic role to the chief as a distributor of valuable goods.

Differences between rich and poor were reflected in their participation in war in still another way. Not owning war bonnets, beautiful head-dresses, or medicine pipes, the poor went to the hills to seek supernatural power for a successful war party, while those who could afford it bought their charms from renowned medicine men. Despite this handicap, informants relate that the poor were the most daring on horse-stealing parties, for they had the least to lose and the most to gain.

Normally, raiding parties started out in the early spring, the summer or the fall, rarely the winter, for the Blackfoot did not like to go out in cold weather. A wise leader would leave at nightfall, travel until dawn, and then rest during the day in shelters constructed in the foot-hills.

The function of the leader consisted mainly in enforcing simple precautionary rules, such as prohibiting a fire for cooking, or the shooting of game once in enemy territory. Every party had one or two scouts who reported to the leader. When the party neared the camp of the enemy the leader decided who was to do the raiding. If the party was small it would break up, every man for himself, and arrange to meet at an appointed spot. In other cases, the leader ordered some to stay, usually the inexperienced or the poorer ones, while the leader, alone or with a choice few, went for the horses. This rear guard duty was resented for there was a possibility that they would not be allowed to share the loot. The chief might present them with a horse, a gift which they were expected to acknowledge at the victory dance.[174] Many parties broke up because of this, those ordered to remain behind often disobeying and going out for their own horses. In cases where the party was mounted and had ambushed the enemy, this individualism was even more marked. It was every man for himself with a great deal of snatching and bickering over the loot, even among brothers.

---

[174] J. Richardson, Mss.

The leader divided the loot, irrespective of whether he obtained the horses or remained behind, provided, of course, that the party had not broken up. If a split occurred, every man retained what he had gotten and there were no recriminations. In the division of the spoils, the leader was guided by the relative age and status of the men and by their part in capturing the horses. It is not clear from the material how these considerations were weighted. In no case did the leader return empty-handed. Unlike the Comanche, the Blackfoot were not content with the prestige of leadership alone.[175]

The return of a successful war party was an impressive event and occasioned general rejoicing and feasting. The party stopped a few miles from the camp, painted their faces, put on their war clothing, and drove quietly to the top of a hill overlooking the camp. "There they would begin the war song, whip the horses to a mad run, and firing guns and driving before them animals they had taken, charge swiftly down the hill into the bottom."[176]

If there were only a few casualties, or if the casualties befell men of little importance or with few relatives, a victory dance would be held, at which there was much exchange of property. Young, unmarried men gave most of their captured horses to older relatives. Since one principle of the division of loot was age, distribution of even a few gifts soon exhausted the loot of the young men. Young men had to go to war from six to ten times before they could accumulate enough horses for an impressive bride price. In giving away their loot they were establishing a source of future credit and aid in joining societies or in raising a bride price. Married men retained more for themselves and went to war less frequently than the unmarried. Scalps given to relatives or friends were repaid by a gift of a buckskin suit or a horse. Modern informants emphasize the trade value of scalps.[177]

The classical view of nineteenth century Plains warfare is that it was in the nature of a sporting game for honor, prestige and scalps. If this were true at all, it was, for the Blackfoot, characteristic of the period before the introduction of the horse and gun, and loot in horses as the dominating motive. Coup was largely ruled out in the parties organized for raiding because of the necessity for stealth and the desire to avoid face to face encounters. While it is true that the capture of a picketed horse rated high as a war deed, it did not compare with the taking of a gun and was not a formal requirement for chieftainship. As a matter of fact, the seeking of coup was confined to defensive encounters where the possibility of loot was

---

[175] See E. Adamson Hoebel, "The Political Organization and Law-Ways of the Comanche Indians," *Memoirs of the Amer. Anthro. Assoc.*, Number 54, 1940.

[176] Schultz, *My Life as an Indian*, p. 47.

[177] J. Richardson, Mss.

necessarily ruled out. Defensive battles were the occasion for a show of bravery, for the capture of guns, shields and bonnets. The prestige derived from the counting of these coup and from the ceremonial recitation of war deeds, though present, was in later years overshadowed by the prestige of wealth.

The relative importance of war honors and wealth can be judged from the fact that bravery and war deeds, the usual requirements for chieftainship on the Plains, though important, were here not essential. There were many chiefs who had never been on the warpath but who had achieved their position by their kindness, generosity, good judgement and wealth.[178] Even a coward, "kopum", one who feared the warpath, could become a chief, provided he had accumulated sufficient wealth to attract followers. By giving frequent feasts, spreading gifts judiciously and buying into the beaver and medicine-pipe societies, any man could gain considerable prestige. This is made more striking when we compare the place of war honors and the counting of coups in Crow life with that among the Blackfoot. The Crow had an elaborate and systematic grading of war honors which was absent among the Blackfoot.

We have indicated earlier that large war parties were used to keep the Plateau tribes out of the Plains. Large parties were also occasioned by two other situations. First, in attacks against the trading posts where the motive was solely loot, and second, when the people felt the death of a prominent warrior or chief at the hands of an enemy as a tribal loss. In such cases, parties were organized in the spring or summer when the bands came together for the Sun Dance. The revenge parties were composed of members of a few bands, rarely of the whole tribe. It is significant that even on these revenge parties, and this applies both to the large and the small, loot was never overlooked.

There were, however, fundamental differences between the organization and motives of the large parties of pre-horse days and those of later ones. The latter were no more than expanded raiding parties. That is, the large party of warriors broke up into small units which acted like the small raiding party intent upon plunder instead of maintaining a unified army under centralized control.

The existence of highly organized warfare among the Blackfoot in the pre-horse period is of special interest in view of the fact that the coming of the horse has become associated in a general way with the development of a high degree of political organization. This process has been shown for the southern Ute of Colorado where the advent of the horse consolidated the small family groups into large bands and transformed a peaceful, retiring

---

[178] A favored son was not expected to go on the warpath but often became a chief.

population into a predatory and dominating people.[179] Much the same process occurred among the Sahaptin people of the southern Plateau and among the Kutenai and Flathead to the east and north. Here, the change was from the small village units to that of large band organizations.[180] In this case, the stimulus for. the changes was the horse, plus the necessity of presenting a powerful front against the tribes of the Plains.

The Blackfoot exemplify a very different process, in which the effect of the horse was to bring about a decentralization in political organization and a fluorescence of individualism. The Blackfoot had already achieved a remarkable degree of political organization in pre-horse times, when the activities of the bands, at least for war purposes, were unified under a central leader.

The concerted action of early tribal warfare was a cohesive force in Blackfoot culture. Far from acting as a unifying factor, the introduction of the horse and gun represented a disruptive one. Later warfare carried on by the small raiding parties became essentially a means of individual aggrandizement in which the tribal interests gave way to those of the individual. Differences between rich and poor became more clearly defined and cut across all institutions. Some chiefs owned thousands of horses while the poor owned none. This developed to a point of incipient social stratification on the basis of horse ownership which resulted in internal disunity.

We can now briefly summarize the more important changes that occurred in warfare as a result of the introduction of the horse and gun and fur trade. The pre-horse motives of warfare, that is, vengeance and the defense and expansion of the tribal hunting grounds persisted, but were displaced in importance by raiding for loot. The religious element in scalping dropped out and scalps were sought for only as trophies of war. There followed changes in organization and tactics. Large massed forces under central leadership gave way to the small raiding party under a temporary leader; open battles with a great show of numbers became less frequent. Instead, stealth, secrecy and ambuscade were employed. Equipment as over against mere numbers became a vital factor. Casualties increased and warfare became a serious and deadly affair.

---

[179] Marvin Opler, "The Southern Ute of Colorado," *Acculturation in Seven American Tribes*, p. 123.

[180] Teit, *Salishan Tribes of the Western Plateau*, pp. 151–152.

VII. CONCLUSIONS

The proposition that the contact with western civilization acted as a stimulus to the development of Plains culture is now well known and generally accepted. Yet we have few detailed studies of this process, and there has been no attempt to solve this essentially historical problem from the historical material. Instead there have been various studies based upon logical and functional analysis of the nature of this process. While some of these speculations show remarkable insight they are no substitute for the actual history.

The development of Plains culture has been discussed mainly in terms of the effects of the horse. Thus Kroeber writes,

" . . . Then about 1650 came the horse which could be taken over with immense profit and without serious readjustment by the bison hunting dogtravois tribes. Population, wealth, leisure increased rapidly and there was a florescence of culture. The material side of life acquired a certain sumptuousness; the warfare of the eastern type was made over into a specialized system with refined social values; rituals and societies multiplied and acquired some magnificence or developed elaborations like age gradings."[181]

Wissler, on the other hand held that post-horse and pre-horse Plains culture were similar in most respects.

How do these views which are meant for the Plains as a whole, compare with our findings for the Blackfoot, a typical Plains tribe? First, our material indicates that the developments so admirably summed up by Kroeber took place approximately 180 years after the date suggested by him, in the case of the Blackfoot. We have seen that the increase in the size of herds, the expansion of polygyny, the borrowing and elaboration of societies and their rituals, and the development of bundle purchases probably occurred about 1830. Nor did all of this follow automatically after the introduction of the horse, for the Blackfoot obtained their first horses in 1730 and were all mounted by 1754.

It is not enough to think of post-horse Blackfoot culture as representing merely an expansion or florescence or earlier conditions. Our study has shown that in the middle of the eighteenth century the Blackfoot made pottery, and baskets, and according to Flathead tradition wore blankets

---

[181] Kroeber, A. L. "Native Culture of the Southwest," *Univ. California Publ. Amer. Archeol. and Ethnol.*, Vol. 23, No. 9, p. 395.

of woven rabbit skins before the time of the horse. On the other hand, the camp circle, considered so characteristically Plains, did not appear until some time after 1754. Warfare was carried on in large groups under a war chief and was a tribal affair. The unified action of the bands in time of war indicates a higher degree of political organization than is usually ascribed to pre-horse Plains.

The fur trade was the mainspring of Blackfoot culture change. The horse alone cannot explain the florescence of Blackfoot culture which took place in the nineteenth century. Rather, it was the fur trade together with the horse and gun which had a dynamic effect upon Blackfoot institutions. The horse without the fur trade would probably have had only the limited effects attributed to it by Wissler for the Plains as a whole. In this sense, the differences between the interpretations of Wissler and Mishkin may reflect objective regional and historical differences between the northern and southern Plains.

In the past the uniformity of Plains culture has also been attributed to the horse. It was argued that with the greater mobility supplied by the horse there was an increase in inter-tribal contacts and an ensuing spreading of culture traits. The role of the fur trade in stimulating this increasing tribal intercourse has hitherto been neglected. We have shown that tribes who formerly had little contact with each other met at trading posts, and have suggested that this was probably the manner in which societies of Mandan and Hidatsa were transmitted to the Blackfoot. Radin has pointed to an analogous process which took place in the Woodlands, whereby the traveling white fur traders were responsible for much of the uniformity which characterizes the Woodland area, and Goldman has shown that the fur trade was instrumental in the diffusion of Northwest Coast culture elements to the interior. It therefore appears that at least three of our culture areas, The Northwest Coast, the Plains and the Woodlands are recent historical products due in large measure to the role of the fur trade as an agent of diffusion.

This study demonstrates both the possibilities and limitations in the use of the recorded history of white contact towards constructing a developmental picture of Blackfoot culture. While we have been able to show the general direction of development of Blackfoot culture, the specific processes are not always discernible. Nor does the material shed light equally on all Blackfoot institutions. Thus we have been able to show process most clearly in the changes in warfare, while the material on economics and social organization is only suggestive of the direction of development. Because there is little reference in the literature to other aspects of Blackfoot culture, such as art and religion, it has been impossible to include them in this study.

APPENDIX

PRE-RESERVE BLACKFOOT RELATIONS WITH THE AMERICAN AND CANADIAN GOVERNMENTS*

United States

The United States government first concerned itself about its western Indians in order to advance American trading interests on the Upper Missouri. When in 1824, Indian agents were appointed for the Indian tribes of the Upper Missouri, they were for the first time within reach of Blackfoot country. It was not until 1834 that an official agent of the government met with the Blackfoot.[1] Indian agents at this time were working in the interest, if not in the employ, of the American Fur Company. Until the 1850's, meetings of Indian agents with the Blackfoot were sporadic. The agents limited their activities to the trading posts where they occasionally distributed goods to the Blackfoot in the name of the Great Father at Washington.[2] There was thus from the beginning an association of the fur companies and the government in the minds of the Indians.

The movement of settlers to the west, which had begun in the thirties reached great proportions by 1850. The increase in the number of immigrants led to plans for the construction of a trans-continental railroad. Before this could be undertaken the inter-tribal warfare between the Blackfoot, Crow, Gros Ventre, Flathead, Nez Perce and Kutenai, had to be stopped. Gov. Isaac Stevens, who headed the railroad survey, therefore began a series of peace councils with the Indians of the northern Plains which led to the signing of the treaty of 1855 with the Blackfoot, otherwise known as the Judith Treaty.[3]

In this treaty Blackfoot territory from the valleys of the Three Forks of the Missouri River, east to the upper waters of the Yellowstone, an area of 30,000 square miles, was set aside as a common hunting ground for the Blackfoot and Gros Ventre. The country north of this common hunting

---

* Since the differential treatment of the Blackfoot by the American and Canadian fur companies was paralleled by their treatment at the hands of the American and Canadian governments, we will trace the relations of the Blackfoot with both governments up to the reserve period.

[1] Chardon's Journal, *op. cit.*, p. 254.

[2] *Ibid.*, p. xxxviii.

[3] A. W. Hoopes, *Indian Affairs and their Administration*, p. 101.

ground as far as the Canadian boundary and east and south as far as the Musselshell River, and north of the Missouri to its junction with the Milk River was defined as the territory of the Blackfoot nation. The United States government was to guard the Indians against whiskey traders, attacks by white men, and any abrogation of their treaty rights. The United States further agreed to spend $20,000 a year for ten years in goods and provisions for the Piegan, Blood and Gros Ventre, and $15,000 each year for ten years to establish and instruct them in agriculture and mechanical pursuits, education and Christianization.[4] This treaty was ratified in 1856.

The Annual Reports of the Indian Bureau indicate that the annuities were peaceably distributed in the years following, but much of the goods received had no relation to the needs of the Indians. One agent wrote,

"I would respectfully recommend that the following be dispensed with altogether . . . calico, ½ of the coffee, fish hooks and lines, combs, thread, . . . and that there be substituted . . . shirts, bed-ticking, flour, powder ball . . ."[5]

These requests were sent in year after year but for the most part went unheeded. There were some feeble attempts to introduce farming and cattle grazing, to which the Indians were definitely not receptive. From 1855 to 1860 there was little change in the conduct of the Indians. The older men tried to abide by the treaty stipulations but the warriors continued on the war path.[6]

Until 1860 the penetration of Blackfoot country by white settlers had been gradual. Routes to the Pacific lay south of the Blackfoot and did not directly affect them. However, the cattle ranching which had been going on near Fort Bridger since the 1840's now began to push north into Blackfoot country. The discovery of gold in 1862 at Grasshopper Creek, within the common hunting grounds of the Blackfoot and Gros Ventre brought still another invasion. Immigrants now came by the thousands and towns sprang up almost overnight. By May 26, 1864, the territory of Montana was created.[7]

There now began a period of bitter conflict between the Blackfoot and the settlers. The low type of American frontiersmen were largely responsible. Of these, General Sully, Superintendent of Indians in the Territory of Montana said, "There is a white element in this country which from its rowdy and lawless character cannot be excelled in any section."[8]

---

[4] *Ibid.*, p. 115.

[5] *United States Indian Affairs Office, Annual Report*, 1857/58, p. 82.

[6] Ibid., 1858/59, p. 116.

[7] Briggs, Frontiers of the Northwest, pp. 161–162, 185–186.

[8] Letter from the Secretary of War, *41st Congress, 2nd Session, H. Ex. Doc. No. 269, p. 3.*

The liquor trade was still rampant, in open violation of the Indian Inter-course Act of 1832 and the Judith Treaty of 1855. Liquor was taking a great toll of Indian lives. The agent at Fort Benton was helpless, but when he objected he was reminded by the citizens "that as they were the advance guard of civilization in the far northwest, barbarians must succumb to their opinions."[9] Given the popular prejudice against the Indians, it was impossible to get a conviction against the whiskey traders in the local courts. "Rather than have a white man punished for assaulting an Indian, the justice of the peace and the sheriff resigned their offices."[10] Violation of government treaties with the Indians concerned them little. "The people claim superior rights to the Indians—and they are indiscriminately killing an Indian when seen,"[11] wrote an agent.

Agent after agent sent annual reports to Washington pleading for a reservation to be set up for the Blackfoot, to avoid the clashes between Indians and settlers. One agent wrote,

"If my services are for good, they are being poorly used while I remain at this place (Benton). It has become a city, duly incorporated as such by the territorial legisla-ture, and has its municipal officers who are unfriendly to the Indians and whose sym-pathies are with the whites in their attacks upon them. If, as I earnestly hope, a reservation will be established for the Blood, Blackfoot and Piegan tribes . . . there may be much good effected throughout this territory. The agent would then be his own master in controlling his agency, without being dictated to as he now is by old trading posts, merchants, thieves, and blackguards."[12]

These pleadings went unheeded until 1874 when a reservation was finally set aside for the Blackfoot.

In the meantime the friction between settlers and the Blackfoot in-creased. In 1865 a treaty was negotiated with the "Blackfoot Nation" in the person of a single Blackfoot chief! The object was to legally open to settlement territory that had already been occupied by the whites. The Blackfoot were to cede all their land lying south of the Missouri.[13]

This treaty was not recognized by the Blackfoot, nor was it ratified by Congress. Immediately after its conclusion the Bloods, Blackfoot and Piegan started to war against the Gros Ventre and the whites.[14] In April, 1866, a party of North Piegan burned the buildings of the government farm on Sun River and continued with an attack on a flourishing cattle ranch nearby.[15] It is significant that the Piegan, until now the most friendly to the

---

[9] George B. Wright, *Annual Report*, 1867/68, p. 256.

[10] *Annual Report*, Sept. 2, 1868, p. 222.

[11] *Annual Report*, July 1, 1867, p. 206.

[12] *Ibid.*, pp. 207–208.

[13] *Annual Report*, p. 13.

[14] *Ibid.*, 1865/66, p. 202.

[15] *Ibid.*, p. 203.

whites, took an active part in these raids. It was their tribal lands that were being invaded by the white settlers (the Blood and Blackfoot ranged north of the line) and they were thoroughly aroused to the danger.

The white inhabitants of Montana viewed the situation with alarm. It was reported that the Blackfoot were planning a war of extermination. "The militia were called out, intense excitement prevailed, but history fails to disclose that these wars ever materialized."[16] What is more, from the Indian agents' reports at this time, we learn that the settlers were on the aggressive. W. J. Cullen, Special Commissioner, who was sent to the Blackfoot, worked to put down the abuses against the Blackfoot. He wrote: "I am risking my life among a set of desperadoes, who live by their wits off the Indians."[17] He tried to prevent a frontier war ". . . which the majority of the settlers appear to be in favor of."[18] Cullen succeeded in concluding a treaty with the Gros Ventre and Blackfoot in 1868. By this treaty all land south of the Missouri was to be ceded to the government in return for which a payment was to be made. The Blackfoot were restricted to the land north of the river up to the Canadian line. The treaty was not to be binding to either party until ratified by the United States government. The failure of the government to ratify it created much discontent among the Piegan. Horse-stealing and petty thieving began again and culminated in the so-called Piegan war of 1869–70.

In the summer of 1869, a few wagons of emigrants were attacked near Fort Benton by Indians, later learned to be the Crow. Just after this, the brother of Mountain Chief, the head of the Piegan, and a young Blood boy, rode into Fort Benton with special orders from Major Alex. Culbertson. They were shot down by the excited settlers. The Piegans were now thoroughly aroused. Major Clark, a former agent of the American Fur Company who had married the daughter of a Piegan chief, was at this time living among the Piegan. A cousin of Clark's wife took advantage of this feeling against the whites to avenge a personal grudge and killed Clark. Four troops of cavalry and 55 mounted infantry under Brevet Col. Eugene M. Baker, started for the Piegan on Jan. 19, 1870. They came upon a Piegan camp whose lodges were filled with sick women and children. Chief Heavy Runner, a friendly Indian, came toward them unarmed and was shot down. The camp was exterminated; 173 women and children were slaughtered and many more wounded. In the investigation which followed, Baker was exonerated and the killing justified.[19]

This massacre, followed by an outbreak of small-pox, effectively and

---

[16] John Carter, *The Blackfoot Claim*, Ms., p. 12.

[17] *Annual Report*, Sept. 2, 1868, p. 222.

[18] *Idem.*

[19] Raymer, *History of Montana*, p. 287.

completely cowed the Piegan. If any resistance on their part had been contemplated, it never materialized. As Curtis wrote:

"A study of the Piegan conflict with the white people, either citizens or soldiers, shows that, considering their number and their provocation, they were one of the most harmless tribes."[20]

Canada

It was not until after 1870 that the Blackfoot felt the force of white expansion in Canada. Blackfoot country had remained free from settlers. The North Saskatchewan, the main highway of traffic to the northwest, was north of Blackfoot country. So long as the Hudson's Bay Company retained its trade monopoly, the Blackfoot were free to continue their old life. But the days of the company were limited. In response to an increasing pressure for a national policy to deal with the growing westward expansion and immigration, Alberta and Saskatchewan were ceded to the Canadian government by the Hudson's Bay Company in 1870.

With the passing of political authority of the Hudson's Bay Company, there came an end to the harmonious relations with the Blackfoot in Canada. A period of free trade now set in.

"New and reprehensible practises in trade were introduced. Competition was keen. Trader outbid trader and upset the century old values fixed by the Hudson Bay Company. Alcoholic spirits, long discontinued by the company . . . for many years now poured in from Red River and from across the border. In southern Alberta, American whiskey runners from Montana introduced the lawless spirit of the American frontier. Contemptuous of Canadian authority, they built forts in Canadian territory, and debauched the Indians with alcohol."[21]

In 1872, Colonel Ross was sent west by the Canadian government to investigate. In his report he recommended that police be sent to put down the liquor trade:

"The demoralization of the Indians and injury resulting to the country from this illicit traffic are very great. It is stated upon good authority that during last year (1871) eighty-eight (88) of the Blackfoot Indians were murdered in drunken brawls amongst themselves, produced by the whiskey and other spirits supplied to them by the traders. At Fort Edmonton during the present summer whiskey was openly sold to the Blackfoot . . . by some smugglers from the U.S. . . .".[22]

In the same year, John McDougall, a missionary, visited the Blood, promising that the whites would soon bring law and order. He later arranged to meet Crowfoot, head chief of the Siksika, and told him that the

---

[20] E. S. Curtis, *The North American Indian*, Vol. 6, p. 7.

[21] Stanley, *op. cit.*, p. 199.

[22] Stanley, *op. cit.*, p. 199.

mounted police were coming to suppress the liquor trade, horse stealing, and inter-tribal warfare.[23] When the Mounted Police arrived they were welcomed by the Blackfoot. The literature contains many speeches of welcome of which the following are typical.

"The Great Mother sent Stamixoton (Col. MacLeod) and the Police to put an end to the traffic in fire water. I can sleep now safely. Before the arrival of the Police, when I laid my head down at night, every sound frightened me; my sleep was broken; now I can sleep sound and am not afraid."[24]

"If the Police had not come to this country where would we be all now? Bad men and whiskey were killing us so fast that very few, indeed, of us would have been left today. The Police have protected us as the feathers of the bird protect it from the frosts of winter."[25]

In 1877, a treaty was signed with the Blackfoot tribes, including the Sarsi, in which provisions were made for them to confine themselves to one large reserve. However, the government thereafter decided upon separate reserves for each tribe. The treaty provided a payment of $12 and an annuity of $5 for each man, woman and child; $25 for each chief and $15 for each minor chief. An annual allowance was provided for schools, ammunition, cattle and agricultural implements.

Comparison and Summary

The tempo of western development in Montana was more rapid and sudden than in Alberta and accordingly, was more devastating in its effects upon the Blackfoot, particularly the Piegan. Long before the disappearance of the buffalo they were hemmed in by cattle ranchers, homesteaders and miners and were ruthlessly pushed off their land. In the ensuing conflict between the Indians and settlers the government with its militia was on the side of the whites. The "bluecoats" became a symbol of a partial government and were heartily feared and hated by the Indians. Treaty after treaty was made with the Indians to legalize the inroads of the settlers, pushing the Indians within more and more confining limits. The Indians were bewildered by the rapid succession of treaties which were often not ratified in Washington and remained mere scraps of paper.

In Canada the Blackfoot fared much better. The later settlement of Alberta, the absence of a lawless frontier class, the prompt and efficient action of the few mounted police in suppressing the liquor trade that cropped up after 1870, and the establishment of reserves for the Indians before the influx of white settlers, spared the Blackfoot the bitter experiences of their American brethren.

---

[23] John MacLean, *McDougall of Alberta*, p. 88.

[24] Stanley, *op. cit.*, p. 203.

[25] A. W. Haydon, *Riders of the Plains*, p. 16.

Considering the strength of the Blackfoot tribes and the number of their grievances in nearly two hundred years of white contact, the absence of any organized resistance or war against the whites is truly remarkable. The literature is replete with statements about threatened uprisings which never occurred. Throughout, conflict with the whites was limited to actions of individuals or a few bands.

On at least three occasions the Blackfoot refused to join anti-white movements. The first was when Sitting Bull fled to Canada after the Custer battle and appealed to the Blackfoot (1877) to join the Sioux in their war against the whites.[26] Later, in 1885, the Blackfoot refused to associate themselves with the rebellion led by Riel, the Cree half-breed.[27] The third was the failure of the Blackfoot to participate in the Ghost Dance movement of the nineties, with its revolutionary anti-white ideology, which was eagerly taken up by neighboring tribes.[28]

This non-participation in anti-white movements is to be understood in the light of a number of considerations. The slower and later influx of white settlers in Canada provided a refuge for the Siksika, Blood, and a portion of the Piegan, for a long time, and gave them a sense of security, though ultimately a false one. Had the Blackfoot tribes been pushed to the wall in the States, without the presence of this Canadian safety valve, they might have offered more stubborn resistance. As it was, it seemed pointless for them to fight American troops when they could still retire to their own land north of the line.

The absence of any well-developed political organization prevented the three tribes from presenting a solid front against the whites and made it impossible for them to utilize the strength inherent in their numbers. The so-called Blackfoot confederacy was a concept used by the traders which had little basis in fact. Despite the bonds of a common language, common customs and traditions and inter-marriage, they rarely acted in unison. They had no common council and no central leaders. Furthermore, within each tribe the bands were highly unstable units. The frequency with which individuals changed band allegiances, was not conducive to successful resistance against the whites, either moral or military.

The days of tribal warfare in defense of hunting grounds were long past. Warfare had become a matter of individual aggrandizement and there appeared to be no motives which would unite the tribes or the bands. In addition to these factors in their social organization and warfare, there was

---

[26] Cecil, Denny, *The Law Marches West*, p. 104.

[27] Stanley, *op. cit.*, p. 361.

[28] The Ghost Dance was taken up by the Assiniboine, Gros Ventre, Northern Cheyenne, Arikara, Gros Ventre (Minataree), Shoshone and Northern Arapaho, see James Mooney, *The Ghost Dance Religion and the Sioux Outbreak of 1890*, pp. 816–817.

the further disruption of their intertribal unity by the fur trade, as was pointed out in the preceding section.

Of no less importance, was the conciliatory role played by the chiefs and headmen, who very often did not consider it to their personal interests to resist the influence of the whites. The early missionaries first commented upon this when they recorded the support they received from the chiefs in their efforts to suppress intertribal warfare and horse stealing. Father Point stated: "Among the Blackfoot, the rich people who undertake to rebuke the wicked who possess nothing, have naught to gain and all to lose."[29] Indeed, peace would insure the security of those who had large herds.

Opposition, both to the cessation of the raiding parties and to the signing of treaties with the whites, came from the younger men. However, they were for the most part, successfully restrained by the chiefs. While it is true that Little Dog, head chief of the Piegan, was killed by his own warriors for his council of peace and friendship with the whites in 1860, Crowfoot, who had much more influence, was successful in keeping down hostile movements against the whites. Crowfoot, who was largely responsible for the maintenance of peace, was motivated by personal, and to some extent tribal, interests. He prophesied the extinction of the buffalo and the ensuing dependence of the Indians upon the whites, and looked upon resistance as foolhardy and hopeless. In 1876, he told Denny, a member of the mounted police,—

"We all see that the day is coming when the buffalo will all be killed, and we shall have nothing more to live on and then you will come into our camp and see the poor Blackfoot starving. I know the heart of the white soldier will be sorry for us, and that they will tell the Great Mother who will not let her children die."[30]

In 1877, he won out against those who counseled against the signing of the treaty. In 1882–83, he allayed the resentment of his people incurred by the putting through of the Canadian Pacific railroad. Without the consent of the other chiefs, Crowfoot secretly capitulated to the railroad for a personal annuity of $700.[31] He was able to mollify the embittered chiefs by judiciously distributing horses. Again, in 1885, Crowfoot used his influence to keep the Blackfoot out 'of the Riel rebellion, but he played upon the fear of the whites to get a promise of larger rations in the future.

---

[29] DeSmet, *op. cit.*, p. 950.
[30] Stanley, *op. cit.*, p. 221.
[31] *Richardson, Mss.*

Selected Bibliography

Sources on the Blackfoot

American State Papers, vol. 2, Washington, 1834.

BELL, CHARLES N. *The Journal of Henry Kelsey (1691–1692), the First White Man to Reach the Saskatchewan from Hudson Bay*....The Historical and Scientific Society of Manitoba, Transactions no. 4 (n.s.), Winnipeg, 1928.

BRADLEY, JAMES H. *Affairs at Fort Benton 1831–1869*. Montana Historical Society Contributions, vol. 3. Helena, 1900.

CARTER, JOHN. *The Blackfoot Claim*. Mss.

CATLIN, GEORGE. *Illustrations of the Manners, Customs, and Conditions of the North American Indians*. London, 1842.

CHARDON, FRANCIS A. *Chardon's Journal at Fort Clark, 1834–1839*....Edited by A. H. Abel, Pierre, South Dakota, 1932.

CHITTENDEN, HIRAM M. *The American Fur Trade of the Far West*. 3 vol., New York, 1902.

COCKING, MATTHEW. *Matthew Cocking's Journal, 1772–1773*. Royal Society of Canada, Proceedings and Transactions, vol. 1, 1907.

COLLIER, JOHN. *Blackfoot Field Notes*. Mss.

CURTIS, EDWARD S. *The North American Indian*, vol. 6, Cambridge, 1909.

DENNY, SIR CECIL EDWARD, bart. *The Law Marches West*. Toronto, 1939.

FRANKLIN, CAPTAIN JOHN. *Narrative of a Journey to the Shores of the Polar Sea, in the years 1819, 20, 21, 22*. Philadelphia, 1824.

GRANT, G. M. *Ocean to Ocean, Sanford Fleming's Expedition through Canada in 1872*....Toronto, 1873.

GRINNELL, GEORGE B. *Blackfoot Lodge Tales: The Story of a Prairie People*. New York, 1912.

HALE, HORATIO. *Report on the Blackfoot Tribes*. Report of the British Association for the Advancement of Science, Sept., 1885.

HAYDON, A. W. *The Riders of the Plains; A Record of the Royal Northwest Mounted Police of Canada, 1873–1910*. Toronto, 1910.

HENDAY, ANTHONY. See Hendry, Anthony.

HENDRY, ANTHONY. *York Factory to the Blackfoot Country; The Journal of Anthony Hendry 1754–1755*. Edited by Lawrence Burpee. Proceedings and Transactions of the Royal Society of Canada, 3rd series, vol. 1, 1907.

HENRY, ALEXANDER, AND THOMPSON, DAVID. *New Light on the Early History of the Greater Northwest. The manuscript journals of Alexander Henry and David Thompson....1799–1814* ... Edited by Elliott Coues, 3 vol., New York, 1897.

HOOPES, ALBAN W. *Indian Affairs and their Administration, with special reference to the far West 1849–1860*. Philadelphia, 1932.

HUGHES, KATHERINE. *Father Lacombe, the black-robe voyageur*. New York, 1911.

HYDE, GEORGE E. *The early Blackfeet and their Neighbors*. Denver, 1933.

KELSEY, HENRY. *The Kelsey Papers*, with an introduction by Arthur G. Dougherty ... and Chester Martin ... published by the Public Archives of Canada and the Public Record Office of Northern Ireland. Ottawa, 1929.

LAROQUE, FRANCIS. *Journal*. Edited by L. P. Burpee. Ottawa: Canadian Archives, 1911.

LARPENTEUR, CHARLES. *Forty years a Fur Trader on the Upper Missouri; the personal narrative of Charles Larpenteur, 1833–1872*; edited with many critical notes by Elliott Coues. 2 vol. New York, 1898.

M'GILLIVRAY, DUNCAN. *The Journal of Duncan M'Gillivray of the Northwest Company at Fort George on the Saskatchewan, 1794–1795*; with introduction, notes and appendix by Arthur S. Morton. Toronto, 1929.

MACLEAN, JOHN (Rev.) *Social Organization of the Blackfoot Indians*. Transactions of the Canadian Institute, 1892.

MASSON, LOUIS RODRIQUE. *Les bourgeois de la compagnie du Nord-Ouest* . . . Quebec, 1889–1890.

MAXIMILIAN, PRINCE OF WIED NEUWIED. *Travels in the interior of North America*. Translated from the German by H. Evans Lloyd, 3 vol., 1843. Thwaites Edition.

MURRAY, GENEVIEVE. *Marias Pass*. Studies in Northwest History, no. 12, State University of Montana. Missoula, 1930.

OLIVER, E. H. The Canadian North-west, its early development and legislative records. . . .2 vol. Edited by Professor E. H. Oliver. Ottawa: Government Printing Bureau, 1914–1915.

RICHARDSON, JANE. *Blackfoot Field Notes*. Mss.

SCHULTZ, JAMES WILLARD. *My Life as an Indian; the story of a red woman and a white man in the lodges of the Blackfeet*. New York, 1907.

SOUTHESK, EARL OF. *Saskatchewan and the Rocky Mountains*. 1875.

TYRELL, JOSEPH BURR. *David Thompson's Narrative of His Explorations in Western America, 1784–1812*. The Champlain Society Publications, vol. 12, Toronto, 1916.

UMFREVILLE, EDWARD. *The Present State of Hudson's Bay*. . . .London, 1790.

United States Department of the Interior, Annual Report, 1879.

WILSON, R. N. *The Blackfoot*. Report of the 57th Meeting of the British Association for the Advancement of Science, 1885.

WISSLER, CLARK. *The Blackfoot Indians*. Annual Archeological Report, 1905, Appendix, Report, Minister of Education, Ontario, pp. 162–178, Toronto, 1906.

——— *Material Culture of the Blackfoot Indians*. Anthropological Papers, American Museum of Natural History, vol. 5, 1910.

Comparative Material

BOAS, FRANZ. "History and Science in Anthropology; A Reply," *American Anthropologist*, n.s., 38: 137–141, 1936.

BLUE, JOHN. *Alberta, Past and Present, Historical and Biographical*. 3 vol. Chicago, 1924.

BRIGGS, HAROLD E. *Frontiers of the Northwest; a History of the Upper Missouri Valley*. New York, London, 1940.

GARDINER, JAMES G. *Fifty Years on the Saskatchewan*. Canadian Northwest Historical Society, vol. 1, no. 5, 1929.

HERSKOVITS, MELVILLE J. *Acculturation. A Study in Culture Contact.* New York, 1938.

HOEBEL, ADAMSON E. *The Political Organization and Law-Ways of the Comanche Indians*. Memoirs of the American Anthropological Association, no. 54, 1940.

INNIS, HAROLD A. *The Fur Trade in Canada; An Introduction to Canadian Economic history*. New Haven, London, 1930.

KEESING, FELIX M. *The Menomini Indians of Wisconsin; A Study of Three Centuries of Cultural Contact and Change*. Memoirs of the American Philosophical Society, vol. 10, 1939.

KROEBER, ALFRED E. *The Arapaho*. Bulletin of the American Museum of Natural History, vol. 18, parts 1–2, 1902.

———— *The Ceremonial Organization of the Plains Indians of North America*. Congress international des americanistes, Quebec, 1907.

———— "History and Science in Anthropology," *American Anthropologist*, n.s., 3: 539–569, 1935.

———— *Natural and Cultural Areas in North America*. Berkeley, 1940.

LINTON, RALPH. *Acculturation in Seven American Indian Tribes*. New York, 1940.

LOWIE, ROBERT H. *Plains Indian Age-Societies*. Anthropological Papers, American Museum of Natural History vol. 11, part 13, New York, 1916.

MANDELBAUM, DAVID. *Changes in an Aboriginal Culture Following a Change in Environment as Exemplified by the Plains Cree*. (In Press).

MOONEY, JAMES. *The Ghost-Dance Religion and the Sioux Outbreak of 1890*. Fourteenth Annual Report of the Bureau of American Ethnology, part 2, pp. 641–1136, Washington, 1896.

OPLER, MARVIN. "The Southern Ute of Colorado," in *Acculturation in Seven American Indian Tribes*. Edited by Ralph Linton. 1940.

RADIN, PAUL. *The Winnebago Tribe*. Thirty-seventh Annual Report of the Bureau of American Ethnology, Washington, 1923.

RAY, VERNE. *Cultural Relations on the Plateau of Northwestern America*. Publications of the F. W. Hodge Anniversary Publication Fund, vol. 3. Los Angeles: The Southwest Museum, 1939.

RAYMER, ROBERT GEORGE. *Montana; The Land and the People*. 3 vol., Chicago and New York, 1930.

SAPIR, EDWARD. "Wiyot and Yurok, Algonkin Languages in California," *American Anthropologist*, n.s., vol. 15, 1913.

———— *Time Perspective in Aboriginal American Culture*, A Study in Method. Memoir 90, Geological Survey of Canada, no. 13, Anthropological Series Ottawa, 1916.

SMITH, MARIAN W. *The War Complex on the Plains*. Proceedings of the American Philosophical Society, vol. 78, no. 3, 1938.

STANLEY, GEORGE B. *The Birth of Western Canada; A History of the Riel Rebellions*. London, 1936.

STEWARD, JULIAN H. AND SETZLER, FRANK M. "Function and Configuration in Archeology," *American Antiquity*, 4: 4–11, 1938–39.

STRONG, WM. DUNCAN. *An Introduction to Nebraska Archeology*. Smithsonian Miscellaneous Collections, vol. 93, no. 10, pp. 1–315, Washington, 1935.

———— "From History to Pre-History in the Northern Plains, in *Essays in Historical Anthropology in North America*. Smithsonian Miscellaneous Collections, vol. 100, Washington, 1940.

TEIT, JAMES A. *The Salish Tribes of the Western Plateaus*. Forty-fifth Annual Report of the Bureau of American Ethnology, Washington, 1930.

TURNEY-HIGH, HARRY HOLBERT. *The Flathead Indians of Montana*. Memoirs of the American Anthropological Association, no. 48, 1937.

VOORHIS, E. *Historic Forts and Trading Posts of the French Regime and of the English Trading Posts.* Ottawa, 1930.

WALLACE, T. A. *The Passes of the Rocky Mountains Along the Alberta Boundary.* The Historical Society of Calgary, 1927.

WISSLER, CLARK. *The diffusion of Culture in the Plains of North America.* Proceedings of the International Congress of Americanists, Quebec, 1906.

———— "Ethnographic Problems of the Missouri Saskatchewan Area," *American Anthropologist,* n.s., 10: 197–207, 1908.